Join one of the world's leading interpreters of Jewish mysticism in discovering why the words of the past reveal the path of our future.

Through wisdom gained from his own forty-year spiritual search for the Divine Presence within, Arthur Green challenges us to question the assumptions of modern consciousness, and by doing so open ourselves to learning from Kabbalah, a profound tool of human understanding.

Drawing on the wisdom of the *Zohar*, the masterwc
tion, and other kabbalistic texts, join Green in exami

- How is the kabbalistic tradition relevant to tod
- Are the ancient and mysterious symbols of any value to us in our very different world?
- How should Kabbalah be refitted so that it might serve as an appropriate vehicle for a contemporary spiritual quest?
- Can this be done without destroying the soul of the tradition and while acknowledging today's reality?

"A well-informed introduction to Kabbalah for the spiritual seeker. It is tremendously refreshing to read a Kabbalah book that draws from the well of Jewish scholarly tradition but also successfully speaks to a larger audience."
—*Publishers Weekly*

"Green's book relays his own spiritual journey and educates the reader along the way. Green is a master teacher, and knows how to develop a point so that the reader is not left behind, but the book demands engagement. This is not a quick read; it is a rewarding one.... Combines the authority of a scholar with the clarity of a teacher."
—*The Jerusalem Post*

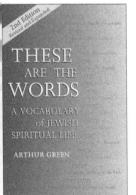

Also by ARTHUR GREEN

These Are the Words, 2nd Edition
A Vocabulary of Jewish Spiritual Life
Teaches about the meaning, history and origin of the core Hebrew words that are shared and understood throughout the Jewish world and why it is important for people to know and use these words in Hebrew.
6 x 9, 320 pp, Quality PB, 978-1-58023-494-8

Judaism's Ten Best Ideas
A Brief Guide for Seekers
An enticing look into timeless Jewish wisdom that will encourage you to explore the riches of Judaism for yourself.
4½ x 6½, 112 pp, Quality PB, 978-1-58023-803-8

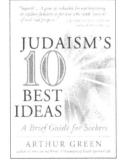

EHYEH

OTHER JEWISH LIGHTS BOOKS BY ARTHUR GREEN

Judaism's Ten Best Ideas:
A Brief Guide for Seekers

These Are the Words:
A Vocabulary of Jewish Spiritual Life

Tormented Master:
The Life and Spiritual Quest of Rabbi Nahman of Bratslav

Seek My Face:
A Jewish Mystical Theology

Speaking Torah:
Spiritual Teachings from around the Maggid's Table
(With Ebn Leader, Ariel Evan Mayse and Or N. Rose)
    Volume 1—Genesis • Exodus • Leviticus
    Volume 2—Numbers • Deuteronomy • The Holiday Cycle

Your Word Is Fire:
The Hasidic Masters on Contemplative Prayer
(Edited and translated with Barry Holtz)

A CONTRIBUTOR TO:
    My People's Passover Haggadah:
    Traditional Texts, Modern Commentaries
    (Edited by Rabbi Lawrence A. Hoffman, PhD,
    and David Arnow, PhD)

אהיה
E H Y E H

A
KABBALAH
FOR
TOMORROW

Arthur Green

JEWISH LIGHTS Publishing

Ehyeh: A Kabbalah for Tomorrow

For information regarding permission to reprint material from this book, please write or fax your request to Jewish Lights Publishing, Permissions Department, at the address / fax number listed below, or email your request to permissions@jewishlights.com.

© 2003 by Arthur Green

Library of Congress Cataloging-in-Publication Data
Green, Arthur, 1941–
Ehyeh: a kabbalah for tomorrow / Arthur Green.
        p. cm.
Includes bibliographical references.

1. Cabala. 2. Mysticism—Judaism. 3. Spiritual life—Judaism. I. Title.
BM525 .G84 2002
296.1′6—dc21

2002013622

ISBN 978-1-58023-213-5 (pbk.)
ISBN 978-1-68336-042-1 (hc)
ISBN 978-1-58023-545-7 (eBook)

Cover Design: Stacey Hood, BigEyedea, Waitsfield, Vermont
Manufactured in the United States of America

Published by Jewish Lights Publishing
www.jewishlights.com

For My Dear Friend and Teacher

הרב משולם זלמן בן שלמה הכהן שחטר־שלומי

Rabbi Zalman M. Schachter-Shalomi שליט״א

My Second Step

Contents

Confession, by Way of a Preface   ·   ix

Introduction: *Ehyeh* as a Name of God   ·   1

PART I: REREADING THE OLD TRADITION

　1 Kabbalah Old and New   ·   9

　2 There Is Only One   ·   19

　3 Torah: Creation's Truth Revealed   ·   29

　4 *Sefirot:* The One and the Ten   ·   39

　5 *'Olamot:* Four Steps to Oneness   ·   61

　6 *Shemot:* The Way of Names   ·   74

PART II: LOOKING TOWARD TOMORROW

　7 Seeking a Path   ·   91

　8 Great Chain of Being: Kabbalah for an
　　Environmental Age   ·   106

　9 All about Being Human: Image, Likeness,
　　Memory   ·   120

10 What about Evil?   ·   138

11 The Life of Prayer   ·   153

12 Community: Where *Shekhinah* Dwells   ·   166

Afterword: To Keep on Learning—Where Do
　I Go from Here?   ·   176

Notes   ·   194

Confession, by Way of
a Preface

THIS BOOK IS WRITTEN FOR SEEKERS. Kabbalah, the ancient esoteric tradition of Judaism, has become of interest to ever-widening groups of willing students, Jews and non-Jews alike. Making this mystical path and its wisdom available in ways that will speak to this new and varied audience is the task that lies before us, and doing so will demand of both writer and reader that we change long-ingrained habits of mind. In writing this book, I have had to overcome the twin fears of revealing too much to the uninitiated and of "watering down" the tradition to the point of trivialization, as it is presented in English and outside its traditional framework. I have gone beyond the bounds of history, taking on the role of teacher to a community of seekers rather than treading the safer and more self-distancing path of historical scholarship. You, as reader, will have to stretch to new ways of thinking, an exercise that involves both heart and mind and, indeed, one that seeks to heal the breach between them that is so much a part of our intellectual life. This book is both a Jewish mystical theology and a work of religious psychology, understanding *psyche* in the original sense as "soul." Through it I hope to speak to you in a deeper and more interior "place" than does most of your reading. Try to read slowly, with the contemplative mind open.

I hope that you will learn a good deal about Kabbalah from reading this book, but its primary purpose is not one of imparting information. Many books, including some very good ones, already exist for that purpose. Instead of just teaching you Kabbalah as it was in the past, I am inviting you to join me in highly contemporary exploration. What does the kabbalistic tradition have to teach today's seeker? Are the ancient and mysterious symbols of any value to us, given the very different world in which we live? How might Kabbalah be refitted so that it can serve as an appropriate vehicle for a very contemporary spiritual quest? Can this be done without destroying the soul of the tradition? Can a thinking person turn to an ancient wisdom source like Kabbalah without fleeing today's reality and abandoning responsibility for life in this world?

A mere generation ago, almost no teachers of Kabbalah could be found outside of a small, closed Jerusalem circle. Today there are too many. Some of them seek to entice students with rosy promises: "Study Kabbalah and all of your problems will be solved! Happiness and success will be yours! Buy our books, drink our special holy brew, and you will be healed of all your ills."

I offer no such promises. I have nothing to sell except my faith in the importance of your inner journey. This is, as I have said, a book for seekers, and I am still a seeker myself. In that the word "seeker" is used to describe a great many people these days, a few words are in order about the one I have in mind as a reader of this book. I assume you are a person of some experience in the spiritual realm. You may have tried meditation according to one method or another. You probably have done some reading on Eastern disciplines and various wisdom traditions. I imagine that you have a sense that some deep truth is hidden in the mystical teachings of Judaism, but do not quite know how to go about gaining access to it. It may well be that you consider yourself a skeptic or an agnostic and yet still are drawn to exploring religious experience and uncovering deeper states of consciousness within yourself. You sense that ancient wisdom traditions, including Kabbalah, may offer you some important tools and insights to help deepen that quest. You may or may not be Jewish by heritage, but have heard of Kabbalah and want to know something of what it has to teach you as a contemporary seeker. You may be new to Jewish practice, or you may be seeking to deepen your own Judaism.[1] You are not looking for a detailed historical account of kabbalistic teaching as it developed in the past, nor are you seeking someone who will try to convince you that Jewish mysticism is the single and only path to truth.

Now I should tell you something about myself. I have been studying and teaching Jewish mystical writings for over forty years. I began as a seeker and remain one to this day. The psalm that says: "Seek God's face always" has come to mean in my own personal prayer-life that the quest itself is endless, that the "face of God" is to be found *within* the seeking, not only as a final goal. Seeking and finding are inexorably tied to one another. The reward for the quest is to be found right here and now, along the path. Trained in the university as a scholar of Kabbalah, it was clear to me from the start that my goal reached beyond the academic, leading toward the cultivation of a spiritual path. The discipline of carefully reading and interpreting texts became very precious to me, however, and served to link the distinct academic and personal pursuits. Over the decades I have come to see myself as a builder of bridges between the scholarly ivory tower, with its great skills in deciphering difficult, obscure sources, and the community of seekers who want to know if there is any value or wisdom in those sources that might still speak to people who live in a very different age from those in which the texts were written.

I have always found it difficult to call myself a mystic. This has something to do with modesty, either real or feigned. (I do not know whether I am *really* a modest person. To ask such a question, and especially to muse about it publicly, is itself a rather immodest thing to do.) Mystics are often thought to be people who have great supernatural religious experiences, who see the room fill with light or the heavens alive with angels. If they write, their tomes are supposed to be filled with great revelations. In our tradition these often come in the form of impenetrable secrets, written in a symbolic idiom that only initiates can understand and that require commentaries by countless generations of disciples. I have no such experiences to share with you, dear reader. I do not consider myself to be an enlightened being, and certainly not one who has escaped and transcended the demands of the flesh. I write on spiritual subjects, as you are about to see, and I do so in a somewhat personal manner. But I try to keep my writing fairly straightforward and "user friendly," perhaps in the hope that greater numbers of people will read the terribly important things I have to say. So much for modesty!

In a certain sense, however, I *am* a mystic, and this book is an admission of it. For all these years, I have been studying, teaching, and receiving most of my spiritual nourishment from the sources of mystical Judaism. I was not more than twenty years old when I discovered Hillel Zeitlin's introduction to Hasidic teachings in his book *In the Garden of Hasidism and Kabbalah.*[2] When he spoke of a world in which only God exists, where everything else is but a "garment" covering the divine light, of raising the sparks of light and serving God everywhere and always, I knew instantly that he was speaking the truth. Not only *the* truth, in fact, but *my* truth. In four decades of a fairly stormy religious life, including lots of ups and downs in my need and ability to engage in religious praxis, this faith has never left me. I knew then, as I do now, that unity is the only truth and that all divisions of reality, including the most primal dualities (God/world, good/evil, male/female, and lots more), are relative falsehoods. That does not mean, I hasten to add, that we can or should live without them.

I have thought a good deal about the genesis of such an intuitive mysticism. Sometimes I have told myself that it arises in infancy, that I belong to an odd group of humans who did not succeed in learning the proper distinction and boundary between "self" and "other." Those who know where the "I" ends and the "Thou" begins can follow Martin Buber or, more in fashion these days, Emanuel Levinas, in philosophies that see reality as so clearly divided between self and other. They can understand truth as proper recognition of the gaps between us and as a series of attempts to bridge them. But I experience Being as a single continuum, a constant flow of energy from the most recondite realms of Divine Oneness into the roots of each single and distinct being, each of us another garb in which the single One seeks to both hide and reveal Itself. And those recondite realms, of course, are not really distanced from each particular person, but are fully present here and now. Present, that is, insofar as we can open ourselves to them.

In this sense I feel that I have not been given a choice. It is only the mystics who tell the truth as I know it. In fact, I prefer a spiritual explanation of this mystical inclination to the psychological one, which I find too simplistic and reductive. Each human being has a divine soul, a part of God, a spark of light, or (if you are not ready for such metaphysical language) a deep longing for Oneness buried within us. That innermost self, the place where each of our individual selves discovers its root in the single Self of the universe, needs to be cultivated, drawn forth from its natural hiding place. The "part" of us that longs for God is an aspect of our most intimate and private person. It is the place where we are most vulnerable, most easily hurt or disappointed. For that reason we hide this aspect of our person, allowing it to come forth only in trusted situations where it is evoked and assured that it will not be harmed. This is the first function of all religious language: calling forth and reassuring that deeper self. Some people seem to have a natural gift for responding to such language and find it easier to open their hearts to that inner dimension. Spiritual discipline is all about training the heart for that response, a way of enabling ourselves to live with our inner doorways just a bit more open, able to respond more freely when we hear "the sound of my Beloved knocking."

I live most of my life, of course, in the same world of separateness and dialogue that we all do. I have no choice about this, either. Life without borders would be impossibly painful, both for me and for those around me. Nevertheless, I have never given up on the faith that it is *wrong*. The most intimate meaning of my prayer-life is bound up with the verse that says, in an old Hasidic interpretation: "the Lord is God in heaven above and on the earth below; there is *nothing* else" (Deut. 4:39). And "on that day," we conclude, everyone will know and bow before the truth that "Y-H-W-H is One and its name One" (Zech. 14:9), meaning that everyone will have the ability to see and name this single truth. Meanwhile, I am forced to pretend, to live here in the world that my teacher Rabbi Nahman of Bratslav called the kingdom of lies.[3] Only he could have told the tale that helps to get me through, day by day:

> Once the king was told that all the crops in his kingdom would be affected by a terrible blight. Anyone who ate of them would go mad. He called in his trusted adviser and asked him what to do. "Of course," the king said, "there is enough grain left from last year's harvest so that you and I could continue eating of it. We would remain sane and keep all the others from doing any harm." "Your majesty," replied the wise man, "if only you and I are sane and all the rest are madmen, who is it that will be locked up in the asylum?" "I understand," said the king, "but what is left for us to do?" "You and I will eat the same grain as everyone else," replied the sage, "but right now I will place a mark on your forehead, and you place one on mine, so that whenever we look at each other we will be reminded of our madness. And that will be enough."[4]

Thank you, Lord, and thank you, rebbe, for making that mark. I still see it quite clearly and I know.

Among the very first pieces I published, just as the 1960s were turning into the '70s, was a pair of essays that gained me a certain notoriety. One was called "Notes from the Jewish Underground: On Psychedelics and Kabbalah." It was published under the pseudonym Itzik Lodzer. (Yes, I am Avraham Itzik, and the great-grandfather who lent me that name came from Lodz in Poland.) The other essay was a "reply" to myself, written a year or two later, called "After Itzik."[5] Today I consider these to be juvenalia and find them slightly embarrassing. Nevertheless, they remain my points of departure. In them I called for a theology that describes the truth as we experience it both at the heights of mystical or psychedelic experience and back here, down "at the base of the mountain." Psychedelics only confirmed for me what I had already seen and tasted in the Hasidic sources. They made the mark a little deeper, harder to eradicate or forget, but they did not put it there. God and the rebbe did that, as I have already said.

By then the importance of *le-ma'an tizkeru* ("so that you remember") was becoming clear to me.[6] The religious life exists in order to keep both the individual and the community in touch with our own deepest moments of experience and insight. We may be destined to live in the valley, but we shape our lives in response to those few and rare moments we have spent on the mountaintop. We Jews call that mountain Sinai, a place and moment sacred to the collective memory of Israel. But it also stands for our own inner peaks, those moments in each of our lives when the border between earth and heaven dissolved and we stood directly in God's presence. How we live, how we love, how we treat one another are all part of our response to those moments.

I have told you most of what you need to know. The rest is indeed commentary. But, as Jews have always known, that is where all the fun lies. I keep trying, in one way or another, to create, offer, preach, teach, bend, bang, and hammer into existence a mystical Judaism that works for me, that gives me a Jewish language in which I can remain faithful to those highest or deepest inner moments. After forty years of struggle I am still banging away. I have not yet come up with any definitive answers. All I have to offer are more—but, I hope, deeper—questions. The struggle with tradition, with Jewish religious language, and with God is my form of commentary. For some reason I am *immodest* enough to think that it might be helpful and interesting to you. Add to all of the above the fact that I am a fellow of rather little natural discipline, but one possessed of a seemingly limitless need for spiritual freedom. I am also burdened by a strong penchant for intellectual and historical honesty. I do not like pretending or fooling myself. Now you may begin to understand why shaping a Judaism that works for me is so difficult, a task that has engaged me across these several decades.

Ah, but you have an answer. "Bend *yourself* more and Judaism less," you tell me, ripe with the wisdom of the ages. "Thank you," I reply. "I'll try."

Meanwhile, I offer these chapters. Still an old revolutionary, I offer them in the hope that reading them will change—or at least challenge—you.

Introduction: *Ehyeh* as a Name of God

KABBALAH TEACHES THAT *Ehyeh* (pronounced *eh-yeh*), or "I shall be," is the deepest, most hidden name of God. It begins with the Hebrew letter *aleph*, which indicates the future tense. When Moses experienced his great moment of calling at the Burning Bush, he asked God: "When the people"—those Hebrew slaves he was about to lead out of Egypt—"ask me 'What is His name?' what should I say to them?" God answers with this mysterious phrase: "I shall be what I shall be," and says to Moses, "Tell them that 'I shall be' sent you" (Ex. 3:14).

God's puzzling answer makes the conversation sound like a koan-dialogue between a Zen master and disciple. "I shall be" as an answer to "What is your name?" seems like a master's slap, a harsh rejection of the question itself. Like the koan, the text here is reaching to some place beyond words, seeking to create a breakthrough in our consciousness. What is it trying to tell us? "I shall be" can mean "I am nameless, because no name could ever grasp who I really am." Or it could mean "Call Me whatever you like. It makes no difference *what* you call Me, because I fill all names—all words, all things, all times and places—and any name you give Me will indeed be mine." The answer becomes a bit clearer in the following chapters as Y-H-W-H, an impossible conflation of the

1

verb "to be," is revealed as God's name. This means nothing less than the truth that God is Being itself. All of Being. *Everything* contains God. There is not a place, not a moment, not a thing, certainly not a person that is not filled to overflowing with the Divine Presence. This is the most essential teaching of the Ba'al Shem Tov (1700–1760), one of the great mystical masters of all time and the founder of Hasidism, a later and more popular version of Kabbalah. The name Y-H-W-H should not be translated "God" or "Lord," but rather "Is-Was-Will Be." It is not really a noun at all, but a verb artificially arrested in motion and made to serve as though it were a noun. A noun that is really a verb is one you can never hold too tightly. As soon as you think you've "got it," that you understand God as some clearly defined "entity," that noun slips away and becomes a verb again.

This name is also considered too holy, too big and powerfully filled with God's presence, to be spoken by ordinary mortals. In ancient times, when the Jerusalem Temple still stood in its place, the high priest alone, after a series of special purifications, was allowed to enter the Holy of Holies but once a year, on the Day of Atonement. Only then was he permitted to pronounce the Name. He did so aloud; we are told that when the Jews who were assembled in the Temple courtyards heard it, they fell on their faces and called out, "Forever blessed be the name of God's glorious kingdom!"

God *is* Being. The four letters of the Name, taken in reverse order, spell the word H-W-Y-H, pronounced *hawayah*, meaning "existence." All that *is* exists within God. But when we turn those letters around and make them into the Name, something of mystery is added. The infinitely varied cosmos gives way to a single Being, One in whose presence we feel ourselves standing, One we allow ourselves to address in prayer. This One addressed in wholeness is infinitely more than the sum of its parts. "God is the locus of the world," the Rabbis teach, meaning that the universe exists entirely within God, "but the world is not God's locus."[1]

God remains transcendent to the universe, a mystery never fully grasped. Y-H-W-H is greater than H-W-Y-H.

The name Y-H-W-H contains past, present, and future. All that was, is, and will be exists in a single simultaneity in God, for the divine embrace is greater than any division into linear time. Only for us time-bound mortals is that division real. All too real, one might add. Most human beings live in the past. Licking old wounds, regretting decisions, and nursing old hatreds occupy a huge portion of the collective energy of humanity. Most of the great human conflicts, between nations as well as individuals, are rooted in such concentration on the past: Jews and Arabs, Serbs and Albanians, Irish Protestants and Catholics, Hutus and Tutsis, child-abusers who were abused when they were children, wife-beaters reliving some ancient terror in their own psyches, and all the rest.

Memory and nostalgia also have their positive aspects, of course. Our lives are made rich, and perhaps somewhat more wise, by the store of memory that increases as the years go by. Hopefully the quotient of old wounds and traumas in our lives is surpassed by the strength of affectionate and warm memories. An inevitable part of adult life is memory, much of it loving memory, of those who have already passed on. But remembering the deceased isn't the only reminiscence to occupy our minds. If we were to divide our minds into the amount of energy we give to yesterday, today, and tomorrow, we would have to admit that a great deal of our mental and emotional energy is devoted to *yesterday*, musing over things that were, that are no more, and that can never be changed.

Today also fills our minds with its demands and concerns. Living at such a fast pace and with so many rival claims on our attention, sometimes we feel we can barely get through the day. The wonderful labor-saving devices that were supposed to give us more leisure seem instead to have made room for even more demands on our time. The newest miracles of worldwide communication make each day more burdensome and keep our minds filled with matters that require instantaneous responses. As the pace of life speeds up, there is a real danger that the human psyche will not be able to keep up with it, effectively making us a society of people constantly oppressed by a burden of demands to which we must attend *immediately.*

But *today* also has a good side. Living in the present means paying attention to *all* that is happening right here and now. The sunlight streaming in the window as I write these words, the clicking of keys on my computer keyboard, the quiet rhythms of my own breathing—to notice all of these is also to notice God, the One that lies behind the many masks of sensation that pass before us in any moment. Spiritual consciousness, according to a wide variety of masters and teachings from around the world, is based on being fully attentive to the here and now. To do so requires the ability to stop, to slow down the pace, and not be overwhelmed by the trivialities of any given moment.

But what of *tomorrow?* Oh, yes, we think about tomorrow. Worry, excitement, anticipation, dread, desire—all of these are the contents of our thoughts about tomorrow. In a word: fantasy. Tomorrow, after all, does not yet exist. How can we think about it other than to fantasize what it will be? But are we really open to tomorrow *as it will be,* rather than as we dream it to be?

Try an exercise:

Quiet your mind by whatever means is familiar to you. Silence, along with attention to your breathing, is always a good, simple choice. As you do so, try to empty your mind of the concerns that weigh on you. Watch them, let them go by, and let yourself become detached from them. Do the same with thoughts, ideas, and plans. Let your mind become as empty as it can, without straining. Turn your attention now toward the future. As you sit quietly, you may want to open your hands, turning palms upward, remaining in silence. The open palms indicate your acceptance. Whatever will come, you will receive

it. Whatever happens tomorrow, there you will look to find
God's presence. "Seek God's face always," says the psalmist.
Always, in whatever happens.

Now you are worshipping God as *Ehyeh,* "I shall be." Note
that "I was" is *not* a name of God. The past is fixed, unchange-
able, set in stone. To worship the past is to serve an idol. *Ehyeh* is
God as future, the One of utter openness to all that is to be. It is
the deepest name of God because it belongs to that stage of being
that the kabbalists call *keter,* the divine crown, or the primal circle. *Keter* is existence that precedes all definition. In the divine
process, to be discussed at greater length in later chapters, but also
in the mystic's own return from the pure contemplative state,
keter is the will to move forward before it has settled into even the
earliest point of defined reality. In *keter,* all is possible and life is
about being utterly open to any and every possibility. We live in
the faith that whatever befalls us, we will find in it a way to discover and rejoice in God's presence. To listen to the God who says
"I shall be" is to surrender the illusion that we are masters of our
own fate. It is to open ourselves and to trust completely. It is not
to trust that any particular result is the one that will occur, but
to trust that whatever the result, the One will be there in it. In
that inner place called *keter,* or *Ehyeh,* we understand that God
loves everything that comes forth (yes, death as well as life; pain
as well as pleasure). Whatever it is, God will be there in it. The
future has a face, say the kabbalists. Even when it appears harsh
and unyielding, we come to accept it as the loving gift of God.
Ehyeh is the divine "face" of unbounded infinite compassion. The
One who loves us is there in all that will happen.

Be open. Have compassion on your own tomorrow. In the
moment when Moses needed to give the slaves an answer that
would offer them endless resources of hope and courage, God
said: "Tell them *"Ehyeh* sent you." The timeless God allowed the
great name Y-H-W-H to be conjugated, as though to say: "*Ehyeh.*
I *am* tomorrow."

PART I

Rereading the Old Tradition

1

Kabbalah Old and New

KABBALAH IN JEWISH HISTORY: A BRIEF SURVEY

KABBALAH IS THE ANCIENT Jewish tradition of esoteric wisdom. The word *kabbalah* itself means "the received," that
which has been handed down and received by us from prior generations. These age-old traditions are said to originate in divine
revelation and are thus "received" ultimately from God. The first
books of Kabbalah began to appear among the Jews living in
Western Europe a little less than a thousand years ago, around the
year 1150 C.E., but the writers and readers of those books saw
them as products of a much older tradition, one reaching back
perhaps another thousand years, into the realm of antiquity.
Modern scholarship, once having scoffed at such claims of ancient
origin, is now becoming somewhat more sympathetic to them.

Kabbalah was passed down for many centuries by a living tradition of master-to-disciple relationships as well as by teachings
first recorded in manuscripts and then in printed books. In the
late fifteenth century, when the printing of Hebrew books began,
many rabbis opposed the printing of kabbalistic works. Since
these sources could only be properly understood if taught by a

true master, the Rabbis thought it better to keep them in manuscript, where only one copy at a time could be created. Preventing mass production through printing was a way of keeping the secrets out of the hands of the uninitiated. Less than a hundred years later, however, the *Zohar* and other great books of Kabbalah began to appear in print, due to the great number of people who sought access to them.

The influence of kabbalistic teachings was at its zenith in Jewish communities throughout the world in the period between 1500 and 1800 C.E. Inspired by the wondrous accounts of the mystics' circles in the Galilean town of Safed, rabbis and preachers began to share the secrets of Kabbalah more openly, and large numbers of Jews—as well as more than a few Christians—became intrigued, seeing in them a source of deep wisdom and ancient truth. In Jewish communities across Europe and the Near East, small groups of men, young and old, created societies for the study and practice of Kabbalah. (Alas, women were excluded from kabbalistic circles in those days.) Their activities included meditation, especially on the secret meanings of God's name, midnight study vigils, processions to honor the Sabbath queen, fasting, ablutions, the chanting of special hymns, and other activities meant to foster an intense life of piety that also would lead toward the redemption of Israel, the cosmos, and even God. Above all, faithful to the learning-centered spirit of Judaism, they studied and mystically reinterpreted the kabbalistic texts, especially the *Zohar*, which itself had achieved canonical status alongside the Bible and the Talmud. They wrote new commentaries on the ancient Scriptures, which were seen as the God-given entrance way to kabbalistic secrets.

KABBALAH AND MODERNITY

As the new winds of modernity and Westernization first began to stir in the mostly self-isolated Jewish communities, some of these kabbalistic groups turned messianic, believing that God was about to bring the Exile to an end. For a century, Judaism was racked by a terrible conflict over the messianic claims of Sabbatai Zevi (1626–1676) and his large following. Partly in response to this crisis, a new type of popular mysticism emerged in Eastern Europe. Known as Hasidism, which essentially means "devotion," this old/new path aimed to simplify the kabbalistic teachings, making them accessible to anyone whose heart was open. The old secrets of cosmology (the study of the structure of the universe) and cosmogeny (reflection on how the world came into being) were now reinterpreted to refer to the life of inner religious faith. Opening yourself to the Divine Presence that is within you and all about you became the immediate goal of this Jewish mysticism. The Hasidim[1] cared little for esoteric lore, seeking only to serve God with joy and wholeness of heart. Redemption was to be found not in the messianic future as much as in the here-and-now of standing in God's presence. This core of early Hasidic teaching, built around the cultivation of religious awareness, was obscured as Hasidism endured its own terrible battles with modernity.

In the nineteenth century, the old worlds of Near Eastern and East European Jewry began to break apart, due to pressures from both without and within. Kabbalah once again became a "hidden" tradition, though this time in a different sense. Jews seeking entree into polite society in the West wanted to show that theirs was a rational and moralistic tradition. Judaism consisted of pure monotheistic faith and biblical morality; it was a religion that could be appreciated by our liberal Protestant neighbors. Kabbalah did not fit into this image and became an embarrassment to the assimilating generations, who came to speak of a "mainstream" Judaism that was a rational form of ethical monotheism, the legacy of the prophets of ancient Israel and the great Jewish philosophers. The message of Kabbalah, addressed to a level of the mind beyond the rational, was pushed to the

margins of Jewish heritage and was either openly mocked or simply ignored and allowed to wither.

Nevertheless, mystical teachings remained alive among small
circles within Jewry. In Europe it was primarily the Hasidic form
of mysticism that survived. Despite the intense pressures of mod-
ernization, the old Hasidic way of life persisted, especially in rural
areas of Poland and in the Carpatho-Ruthenian region on the border of the Ukraine and Hungary. For many, of course, this way of
life was simply traditional, and holding fast to it was a statement
of loyalty to tradition and the teachings of prior generations. New
Hasidic writings continued to appear, however, and religious devotion in its most intense form could be seen in the groups of disciples who gathered around the Hasidic masters in these areas
and, increasingly as years passed, in the Holy Land as well.

Among Sephardic or Near Eastern Jews, kabbalistic knowledge also survived in small circles, especially in Jerusalem and in
such Diaspora communities as Iraq, Turkey, and Morocco. In
these settings, the more pure forms of kabbalistic wisdom were
combined with popular traditions and aspects of folk religion.
Mystical sages and holy men were venerated in Morocco just as
intensely as they were among the Hasidim of the Ukraine. Tales
of miraculous healings and supernatural powers of the righteous
became part of the stock-in-trade of mystical teachers. Needless
to say, these were precisely the kinds of tales that were most de-
cried by leaders of Jewish modernity. No wonder that the first
generations of Near Eastern Jews to attain modern education,
like their earlier counterparts in Europe, sought to leave the mystical tradition behind.

About a hundred years ago, when Kabbalah and Hasidism appeared sufficiently vanquished, no longer threatening "progress"
into the Jewish future, a few daring seekers began to question
Jewry's flight from this innermost part of its spiritual legacy.
Modern figures such as Martin Buber (1878–1965), Hillel Zeitlin
(1871–1942), and Jiri Langer (1894–1943) turned back to the mys-

tical tradition, mainly through Hasidism, and wrote of it in a loving way. Their somewhat romantic re-creation came to be called neo-Hasidism, and it found deep expression in the literature and artistic creativity of Jews throughout the twentieth century. A few decades later, largely thanks to the efforts of Gershom Scholem (1897–1982), university-trained scholars began to examine the texts of the mystical tradition, allowing the modern seeker access to sources containing ideas and practices that had been neglected for centuries.

The terrible traumas of destruction and dislocation that visited Jewry in the middle of the twentieth century nearly obliterated the few remaining pockets of mystical practitioners. Hasidism in Russia was destroyed by the Communist regime beginning in the 1920s. The Hasidim in Poland were almost totally wiped out by the Nazis, who took special delight in torturing these "most Jewish" of all their Jewish victims. Such leading voices of Hasidic and neo-Hasidic creativity as Rabbi Kalonymos Shapira of Piasecne (1889-1942) and Hillel Zeitlin were among the victims of the Warsaw ghetto, and thousands of other masters and faithful disciples were slaughtered all over Eastern Europe. Near Eastern and North African Jews, while mostly escaping the Holocaust, shared with their surviving European brethren the years of dislocation and adjustment that led many to abandon tradition in the struggle to get ahead in new homelands and settings.

For many, of course, that new homeland was the Jewish State. It probably could have been predicted that the return to Zion would lead to the renewal of the Jewish mystical spirit as well. There had always been a strong link between the Holy Land and mystical teaching. The difficulty of life in Israel, and especially the need to find meaning in the great sacrifices required and to search for legitimization of Israel's claims to the land, have led quite a few Israelis directly back to kabbalistic tradition in one form or another. In the last quarter of the twentieth century and the first few years of the twenty-first we have witnessed a tremendous growth in the spread of mystical ideas and practices—both within Israel and around the world—by oral teaching, publication of new books, the printing of once-obscure manuscripts, and by electronic means not even dreamed of by prior generations of the faithful.

KABBALAH TODAY: DANGERS AND HIGH HOPES

As a Western Jew who has spent most of his life attracted to the mystical spirit within Judaism, I look upon this revival with a mix of emotions. It is wonderful to see the old books being printed and studied again: the translations, the new commentaries and publications, and the many primers on Kabbalah in Hebrew, English, and other languages. The cultivation of spiritual consciousness among Jews is a goal I fully share with the growing numbers of kabbalists in Jerusalem and elsewhere. I cannot but be excited by the growth of worldwide interest in a realm of study to which I have devoted so much of my own life.

At the same time, I understand the power of mysticism well enough that I also fear it. Mystical consciousness is powerful and seductive. Its ecstasies can threaten critical thought in areas where reason and realism are truly needed, especially in politics and relations between Jews and other ethnic or religious communities. Kabbalah has long been associated with a certain xenophobic stream within Jewish thought, one that sees Israel's covenant with God in terms of unique qualities of the Jewish soul or declares that Jews alone have the capacity to respond to divine revelation. Some have used these teachings to delegitimize other faiths, viewing them as inauthentic because they are not rooted in divine revelation. Mystical glorification of "the souls of Israel" can also be construed to infer a Jewish spiritual "superiority," and thus to denigrate the humanity of others. Such thinking was understandable in the long centuries of Jewish suffering and victimization. Perhaps feelings of superiority were necessary for the spiritual survival of the Jewish people in the face of demoralization. Ultimately such feelings are deeply misguided, however, and they do not represent Judaism at its best: the place where it is most faithful to its own great assertion that *every* human being is created in the image of God and that God is wise and mysteriously transcendent, beyond any exclusive human grasp.

Contemporary seekers need to carefully consider certain other aspects of the old mystical tradition before accepting them. Like most forms of mysticism, Kabbalah and Hasidism cultivated tales of great masters and their wondrous powers. The naive imagination of devotees typically exaggerated such accounts, claiming miracles, healing powers, and this-worldly rewards for mystical practice that strain the modern reader's credulity. These claims may be appreciated for a certain charm, but they should not form the basis for a contemporary revival of Jewish mysticism. We would do far better to remember the ancient Rabbis' teaching that "the reward for a good deed is the good deed itself" and their warning that we should not be "like those who serve the Master in order to receive a reward."

I, too, look toward a revival of the Jewish mystical spirit in our age, but for me, this has to represent Judaism in its broadest, not its narrowest, vision. Our return to Judaism is indeed connected to our return to the Land; that mystery cannot and should not be denied. Yes, *we*, the entire Jewish people (including those who choose to live abroad) have returned to the Land. We have rediscovered a *place* that we love and that calls to us as deeply as do the sacred *moments* of our tradition. This has helped us to redress a certain overspiritualization, a lack of attention to the earth and to the body, to the physical grounding of the spiritual life, that had developed over centuries of wandering. In this sense the recovery of Kabbalah is a fully Jewish event, a part of the Jewish people's history in this unique time.

TOWARD A POST-MODERN MYSTICISM

There is also a universal and environmental element growing directly out of this return to the Land that is essential to our Kabbalah for tomorrow. We need a new *this-worldly* piety in Judaism and in all religions, an attitude fitting to an environmentally concerned future that is already upon us. I seek in a contemporary Kabbalah a Judaism unafraid to proclaim the holiness of the natural world, one that sees Creation, including both world and human self, as reflecting divinity. I seek a Judaism that looks to nature itself, with its wonder, mystery, and beauty, as a source of religious inspiration. I long for a Judaism that teaches us how to live in harmony with the natural world, one whose most basic teachings will demand of us that we position ourselves at the cutting edge of sensitivity toward relieving the suffering and pain of all God's creatures. God's name is inscribed in all that is. To take for granted the endless material gifts with which we are blessed is to take God's name in vain. To degrade another human being is to diminish the Divine Image; to stand by as though unaware of his or her degradation is to shut our eyes to the image of God. But we must also learn to read the imprint of God in the rest of Creation, in animal and plant life, in all their infinite and now much-threatened diversity, in such simple but essential gifts as soil, air, and water. It is partly in this spirit that I turn to Kabbalah, and especially to Hasidic teachings, seeking to learn from them as they were in the past, but also to adapt and transform their vision for the unique times in which we live.

Kabbalah as a grand system of truth, one that encompasses all reality and could answer all our questions, belongs to the past. In that role it gave way to the competing world-view of experimental science nearly three hundred years ago. Science and its discoveries brought forth the modern world and all its great advances, including many in the social and political realms, as well as within the natural sciences. Today we live in a world that is often described as *post-modern*. By this we mean that our age is open to challenging and questioning certain assumptions of the modern consciousness. We are less confident about the steadiness of progress in many areas of human endeavor than were the immediately preceding generations. We question whether science is the right way to pursue some of our great and eternal questions about life's purpose. In this context, we seek to reexamine the more profound tools of human self-understanding that were cast aside with the advent of modernity. Kabbalah is one of these, and in this spirit we open ourselves to learning from it.

But let us be clear. *Post*-modernity is not a return to *pre*-modernity. All the grand systems of metaphysical truth taught by prior ages collapsed for good reason. In turning back to the sources of Kabbalah, we seek inspiration and wisdom for what is essentially a Jewish mysticism for a post-kabbalistic age. We seek to be richly nurtured by the past, but not to return to it or to restore its unquestioned authority. In that sense, our work continues that of the neo-Hasidic teachers who came before us, mining the deep veins of spiritual insight within Judaism for use by those living in a different age and with very different sets of life experience.

The old Kabbalah suffered the limitations of the Diaspora Jewish society that created it. Living either in urban ghettos or impoverished shtetls, Jews had relatively little appreciation of the natural world and its mysterious beauty. Unlike the psalmists and prophets of antiquity, who saw all of Creation as living testament to the greatness of God, the inner life of Diaspora Jews often tended toward abstract thought and evermore subtle forms of argumentation. Codes of moral law and religious praxis became the bread and butter of intellectual activity on which the Jewish community staked its survival. The *Zohar*, a work of dazzling poetic beauty, is very much an exception to this tendency. Its pages are filled with images of rivers and mountains, streams of light, and hidden gardens that all point to the secret inner life of divinity. The lush imagery of the Song of Songs, providing a heady mix of natural

beauty and sensuality, pervades the work. Later kabbalists re-
treated once again from this engagement with the natural world,
returning Kabbalah to the realm of abstraction. Nevertheless,
there are important reasons why a contemporary Jewish religion
of nature should anchor itself in the mystical tradition.

2

There Is Only One

GOD ABOVE, GOD WITHIN

T HE BASIC TEACHING OF MYSTICS, dressed in the garb of many
traditions, is essentially this simple message: There is only
One. All multiplicity of beings and their sense of separateness or
distance from one another are either illusion or represent a less
than ultimate truth. This is especially the case, in the language of
Western mysticism, in the great alienation or sense of distance
that humans feel between themselves and God.

To open our discussion of Judaism from a mystical perspective, we turn to a famous parable of the Ba'al Shem Tov:

A great king sought to test his beloved son, to see if he would
truly seek him out. He created the optical illusion of a beautiful
palace. All who came to see the king, it was announced, would
have to come through that palace. One person came to see the
king and got only to the outer courtyards. There he came upon
barrels of silver coins, glistening in the sunlight. They were so
beautiful that he turned aside to gaze upon them and to touch
them. He is there still, playing with his silver coins. Another was

stronger, and he traversed the outer courtyards until he came to the chambers within. But there he found vessels of pure gold so lovely that he could not take his eyes from them. He is there to this day, staring at the gold. One by one the visitors were turned aside by the beauties of the palace. But then the king's true son came along. He saw immediately that the palace was all illusion, that there was nothing there but the king himself.

Kabbalah teaches that there is a secret unity of all Being, hidden within the multiplicity and diversity of life as we experience it. God and universe are related not primarily as *Creator* and *creature*, which sounds as though they are separate from one another, but as *deep structure* and *surface*. God lies within or behind the facade of all that is. In order to discover God—or the real meaning or the essential Oneness of Being—we need to turn inward, to look more deeply at ourselves and the world around us. Scratch the surface of reality and you will discover God. The path to God is thus more like peeling off the layers of an onion than climbing a ladder to the sky. The "journey" of the seeker to God is only a metaphoric one. We, in fact, discover the Oneness of Being by staying right *here,* paying as close attention as we can to the present in which we live. But if we are to speak of journeys, the mystic offers us a journey inward, an inner opening rather than a vertical ascent.

Throughout its history, Judaism has been engaged in the struggle between these two root metaphors, the vertical and the internal. As spiritual descendents of ancient Semites who (long before the Bible) worshiped gods said to dwell in the sky, our most natural tendency is to think of the relationship between God and world as that of "heaven" and "earth," or to put our theological concepts in *vertical* terms. There is much in the Bible and the traditional language of Judaism that reinforces this way of thinking. The account of Sinai itself may be seen as a *vertical* story, where God "descends" onto the mountain as humans struggle to reach its top. So too Jacob's dream of the ladder reaching from earth to heaven, the Tower of Babel, and many more.

Another passage within the Torah itself seems to challenge that view. As Moses finishes summing up his teachings before his death (this series of "speeches" comprises the entire biblical Book of Deuteronomy), he says to Israel:

> The commandment which I give you this day is not too wondrous for you, and it is not far away. It is not in heaven, lest you say: "Who will ascend to heaven to fetch it for us and allow us to hear it, that we might do it?" It is not across the sea, lest you say: "Who will cross the sea for us to fetch it for us and allow us to hear it, that we might do it?" This thing is very close to you, in your own mouth and your own heart, that you might do it (Deut. 30:11–14).

What does the Torah mean here? It does not sound as though Moses is saying: "God's teaching indeed *used to* be in heaven, but I have already brought it down for you!" This seems to be a rather different Moses than the one who climbs the mountain. Here he seems to be telling us that the journey to Torah is, and always has been, an inward rather than a vertical journey. The only place you have to travel to find God's word is to your own heart. The journey to the heart is the mystical quest.

God and world are deep structure and surface of the same reality. This means that knowing God, knowing the world, and authentic self-knowledge are all aspects of the same search for truth. The same is true on the plane of emotion: love of God, love of all creatures, and proper self-love cannot be separated from one another. To worship God is to live with reverence, to treat all beings, including oneself (this is often the hardest part!) as embodiments of the single Being, called in Hebrew *alufo shel 'olam,* the cosmic *Aleph,* or the single One.

THE ONE AND THE MANY

Because Kabbalah speaks to us of a hidden unity that we cannot ordinarily perceive, its language can sometimes be confusing.

Statements that seem to be in conflict stand side by side with one another. The mystic mind understands that there are truths that can be expressed only by paradox. Seemingly contradictory expressions of "on the one hand" and "on the other hand" actually mean that both "hands" belong to the same Being and are true at one and the same time. *Eyn Sof* ("The Endless," a term used for the most mysterious and unknown Reality) is all; the One is without limit and without end. There is no being but the one Being. But "on the other hand," the reality of *Eyn Sof* is so deep and seemingly remote from ordinary consciousness that we have to go through stages of development in order to "get there." Much of Kabbalah is devoted to describing these stages, training the mind to open to this simplest but most elusive of all truths.

One of the most creative teachers brought forth by Hasidism in the later nineteenth century was Rabbi Judah Leib Alter of Ger (1847–1904), author of the *Sefat Emet*.[2] Many of the Torah interpretations offered in that work turn to the essential themes of mysticism: seeing beyond the surface, the nearness of God, and the oneness of all existence. But nowhere in all those teachings does the teacher speak quite so directly as he did in a letter to his children and grandchildren, telling them the meaning of the *Shema'* ("Hear O Israel") and the reason we recite it every day:

> The proclamation of oneness that we declare each day in saying "Hear O Israel," and so forth, needs to be understood as it truly is. That which is entirely clear to me...based on the holy writings of great kabbalists, I am obligated to reveal to you...the meaning of "Y-H-W-H is One" is not that He is the only God, negating other gods (though this too is true!), but the meaning is deeper than that: there is no being other than Him. [This is true] even though it seems otherwise to most people...everything that exists in the world, spiritual and physical, is God Himself. It is only because of the contraction *(tsimtsum)* that was God's will, blessed be He and His name, that holiness descended rung after rung, until actual physical things were formed out of it.

These things are true without a doubt. Because of this, every person can attach himself [to God] wherever he is, through the holiness that exists within every single thing, even corporeal things. You only have to be negated in the spark of holiness. In this way you bring about ascents in the upper worlds, causing true pleasure to God. A person in such a state lacks for nothing, for he can attach himself to God through whatever place he is. This is the foundation of all the mystical formulations in the world.[3]

The "foundation of all the mystical formulations in the world" is the realization that God is everywhere, indeed that nothing but God exists. This leads us to the great question of mysticism, asked in one form or another in each of the mystical traditions. "Why is it that we do not experience the world this way?" If God is all, why do separations and distinctions between one thing and another, especially the basic separations between self and other, God and world, seem to be so real? If the mystic's unitive vision does represent reality, what is the relationship between that truth and the multifaceted, differentiated world in which we seem to live?

The kabbalists' answer to this question will take us to the heart of Jewish mystical teaching, the *sefirot*. These ten primal realities are the stages by which God is revealed, constituting the true inner structure of all reality. The kabbalist sees the many emerging from the One in subtle and sometimes imperceptible ways. The One underlies the many, which emanate or flow forth from it. In a very gradual (paradox: but also both instantaneous and constant) process, the endless God emanates or flows into each form of being. The primary stages of this "great chain of being" are of particular interest to the kabbalist, especially because they involve the various inner layers of the godhead and the evolution of God from deep and hidden mystery into the images in which "He"—and sometimes "She" as well—is usually depicted. The kabbalist, in other words, is concerned precisely with

the question many of us were told not to ask when we were cu-
rious youngsters: Where does God come from?

In the beginning there was only One. There still is only One.
That One has no name, no face, nothing at all by which it can be
described. Without end or limit, containing all that will ever come
to be in an absolute, undifferentiated oneness, that reality can
only be referred to by a negative phrase: *Eyn Sof,* "that which has
no end." *Endless* is the first, and in some sense the only, thing one
can say about this most primal mystery of Being.

Eyn Sof includes all that ever was, is, will be. All of this is
united in a state that does not yet distinguish "potential" from "actual," the realizable from the real. It represents a fullness of energy beyond all description. Out of that energy comes forth all
that is, a transforming explosion that in each instant makes the
full journey from Being to beings, from the infinite mystery of
Y-H-W-H to the infinite realities of existence.

Why does that explosion take place? Why did, or does, Being
emerge from the "black hole" that precedes existence? To answer
such a question would be to say more about *Eyn Sof* than we can.
"Will" and "desire" are concepts far too human for us to project
onto the "face" of faceless mystery. Perhaps "anticipation" is a
slightly more neutral term. The first stirring within the One that
leads toward the existence of the many is the sense of time, a
drawing forth of the future from within the timelessness of
Being. As the potential examines itself (and how could *Eyn Sof* not
be self-reflexive?) and realizes its own potency, the thought
emerges of a *future* in which that potential might be realized.
Thus is born a linear sense of time, a sequential before-and-after
that pulls forth from the closed timeless circle of *Eyn Sof.* It is
here that we speak of *Ehyeh* or *keter* revealing itself from within
Eyn Sof, the first stirring of that which will become the multiplicity of existence.[4] It is of *Ehyeh,* or God-as-future, that Scripture
says "Draw me after you, let us run," in the love-language of the
Song of Songs.

TSIMTSUM: THE SELF-CONTRACTION OF GOD

This moment of Being realizing its potential was also discussed by the later kabbalists (Rabbi Isaac Luria and his followers) when they taught the mystery of *tsimtsum*, the divine "contraction" or the self-limitation of *Eyn Sof*. The first dawning of the future, with its possibility of a "drawing forth" of energy into the realm of multiplicity, immediately raises the question of "otherness" to *Eyn Sof*. If the Endless is truly without end—without limits or borders of any sort—is there any way in which any other being can be said to exist? Of course, the most radically mystical answer is "No!" The assertion that all claim of the non-God to existence is spurious. The kabbalist understands this and, in the deepest recesses of his own being, knows it to be true. *Eyn Sof* remains just that. The mystic who knows this is the one who hears Moses saying, "Know this day and set it upon your heart that Y-H-W-H is God in heaven above and on the earth beneath; *there is nothing else*" (Deut. 4:39). But that same kabbalist also has a commitment to the reality of this world. God has not brought us into existence as disembodied spirits, but as minds and bodies, replete with ego-needs and limitations. There must be a reason why we were created with individual consciousness and a sense that each of us is a distinct and separate self. The task that we have to do in this world (named both as "the world of separateness" and "the world of lies" by the kabbalists) calls upon us to take ordinary consciousness and worldly existence seriously.

In order to allow for that to happen, for the separateness of "Creation" from God to have a modicum of reality, *Eyn Sof* has to hold itself back, withdrawing, as it were, to create a primal void, within which the "other" can begin to take shape. This is the kabbalistic notion of *tsimtsum*. God withdraws from a certain dimension of reality in order to allow the non-God to exist. According to some kabbalists, this process of withdrawal is happening constantly, allowing for the renewal of existence and the appearance of new life forms in each moment. God always has to withdraw in order to create, to allow room for the "other" to be.

Tsimtsum is a profound and challenging idea, but it also raises as many questions as it answers. One of these questions goes to the very possibility of imagining anything truly outside of God. How does the withdrawal of divine energy take place? Is it not God who does it? In fact, God withdraws out of love, seeking to make room for the other to exist. If so, the void itself is a divine creation, one that must contain God's presence just like anything else that God creates. But if the void is created by God and contains God's presence, it really is no void at all! Thus there can really be no void and therefore no existence outside God. Our sense of "otherness" is but illusion.

Some mystical teachers, especially among the Hasidic masters, try to finesse this problem by suggesting that *tsimtsum* takes place in the mind rather than in outer reality. "Creation" is, in fact, nothing but a *hiding* of the ever-present divine light behind successive veils, making God's presence invisible to the untrained human psyche. God as loving parent or teacher does not want to overwhelm the childlike human mind by revealing too much of the radiant oneness of Being. As the child learns and trains toward greater maturity, the veils are removed, one after another. It is in the life of contemplative prayer, in the discipline of religious practice, and in the study of Torah with a kabbalistic eye that we train ourselves to see more of the divine reality within us and all about us. From God's point of view, as it were, there has been no *tsimtsum*. The divine light shines everywhere and all of us are but refractions of its glow. This truth needs to be hidden from us until we become ready to absorb it. As we train ourselves step by step, over the course of a lifetime of growing awareness, more of that light is revealed to us.

CREATION: THE MYSTICS' VIEW

As pious Jews, the kabbalistic and Hasidic masters always affirmed their faith in Creation. God is the source of all that exists and all has been created out of God's love. Their understanding of Creation, however, goes beyond the standard biblical and rabbinic teaching in three important ways.

We have already referred to the first of these. Creation begins not with the material world, but with the emergence of the knowable, personal God out of the mystery of Divine Oneness. The pattern in which this emergence happens is that of the *sefirot*, the essential "story" of all Kabbalah. The creation of the lower world is but a repetition of the pattern, one in an endless series.

The *ongoing* nature of Creation is also of great importance to the mystical tradition. The Rabbis had already taught this by including the line: "Each day God renews the act of Creation" in the daily morning service. Creation is not a distant one-time event, nor is it a formal theological doctrine to which one must give adherence. Creation may be *experienced* each day, indeed in every moment. The Hasidic masters insist that only a person who feels like a new creature each morning is truly able to recite the prayers. Otherwise prayer is just habit, the enemy of a true, dynamic faith.

In each moment, God creates the world again. The first moment of Creation sets forth the paradigm of God as Creator. In Hebrew we often refer to God as the *Boré 'Olam*, Creator of the world. This name for God reflects the present tense, God the ever-creating. From the point of view of faith, this is what it means to know God in Creation. We find signs of Divine Presence throughout the world. We recognize the handiwork of God both in the wonders of nature and in the miracle of our own ability to be stirred by those wonders. We turn toward the Source of all life to express our gratitude for existence. This is how we stand before God as Creator.

The third pillar of the kabbalists' view of Creation is their insistence that God creates out of God's own self. The flow of energy by which Creation happens comes directly from God. When the mystics encountered the old theological formula claiming that God creates the world *yesh me-ayin*, "out of nothing," they agreed, saying that God is the No-thing out of which Creation comes!

Here the idea of Creation has essentially been reread as one of *emanation*. God is the inner source or fountain out of which all existence flows. God is eternal and hence preceded Creation and caused it to happen. But the more important part of the teaching is that God is always present, within and behind the world as we know it, sending forth the renewing surge of energy from within the deepest recesses of God's own self.

3

Torah: Creation's Truth Revealed

HOKHMAH: TORAH BEFORE LANGUAGE

JUDAISM IS GENERALLY UNDERSTOOD as a religion of revelation. Its claim is that God revealed the Torah to Moses on Mount Sinai, choosing Israel as the people to fulfill the divine will by living in accord with God's commandments. All the rest of Judaism, according to this intentionally oversimplified picture, is the spelling out of that will.

But this is a Judaism of biblical literalism. It does not nearly express the Judaism of the Rabbis, whose teachings embody significantly more complex and nuanced understandings of revelation. To begin with, they claim that Torah did not come into being just as God spoke it to Moses and Israel. Torah is not just the message of Sinai, but the eternal Word of God. It was there from the great beginning: Torah existed before the world was created. In fact, says the opening midrash (rabbinic commentary) on the Book of Genesis: God looked into Torah and created the world.

This faith in primordial Torah underlies both Judaism and Christianity. Torah is identical with the Word of God, the word or the power of speech by which God created the world. For Christianity, this is the Word that "became flesh" in the Incarnation of Jesus Christ. For Judaism, the Word remains forever Word, given to Israel at Sinai and realized in the deeds of all those who live the life of Torah. In a certain sense, no person can be the living incarnation of God's Word, and in another sense we *all* are potentially just that.

What do we mean when we refer to a Torah that existed before the world itself? The Torah as we have it is a rather worldly and human document. It begins with Creation but then proceeds quite quickly to tell the tale of human history. Could it be that the account of all the generations of Genesis and all the tribes of Israel was written in the Torah before any of them lived? What then happens to the spontaneity of history and to the all-important doctrine of free will that makes for human responsibility? Could it have been written before Creation that God would harden Pharaoh's heart? Or that Israel would make the Golden Calf? That Zimri would sin and that Phineas the Priest would kill him? It hardly seems to make any sense.

Another question: just what does the notion of "writing" before Creation mean anyway? The Rabbis long ago noted that no parchment, quills, or ink existed before Creation. How then was the Torah written down? They suggest that it was written "in black fire on white fire," a way of trying to express something entirely supernatural about the notion of primordial "writing." We would add that writing itself is a human invention. Indeed, so is language. No humans before Creation, no language without humans. But what is Torah without language? What could we possibly mean by a contemporary notion of primordial Torah?

When the tradition speaks of Torah in this way, it often quotes verses from Scripture that refer not to Torah but to *hokhmah,* or Wisdom. Wisdom "speaks" in the verses of the Books of Proverbs and Job, claiming that "she" was with God from the beginning, that she was "His" delight before all else came into being. As we will soon see in our discussion of the *sefirot, ḥokhmah* is the be-ginning of God's way, the primal point of all existence. Sometimes it is described in Kabbalah as the deep well out of which will bub-ble forth the spring of life. The kabbalists follow very ancient teachings in their claim that *ḥokhmah* exists deep within the mind of Being, the first concretization of the will that makes for exis-tence. It is far beyond language, and one can contemplate going there only in total silence.

The notion of primordial Torah could then mean that the *in-tent* to bring about existence, including all its many forms and even a humanity that would quest for understanding, was all there from the beginning. The evolutionary process that brought all creatures into existence is constantly striving toward a single goal. That goal is the ever fuller self-manifestation of the One, the Source of Being, that undergoes this long dance of evolution, until reaching the minds of those creatures. We, the products of that evolutionary process, are constantly advancing in our compre-hension and appreciation of the world in which we live. *Ḥokhmah,* or the "Wisdom of God," is the *comprehensibility* of existence, the potential for life's meaning to become revealed to the seeker's mind.

THE TEN PRIMAL WORDS

Primordial Torah is associated with the Mishnah's claim that "with ten utterances was the world created."[1] Ten times in the first chapter of Genesis, according to this view, God says: "Let there be!" (*Yehi*—"Let there be"—in Hebrew is a verb that is re-lated to the name of God, Y-H-W-H.) These ten utterances are spoken not once, but eternally, the Word of God that forever stands as the basis for being in all its forms. In each moment of existence, "Let there be!" is flowing forth from its divine source. The infinite variety of all life branches forth from these ten di-vine surges of energy that underlie and vivify all reality.

The point of this teaching is that God is present throughout Creation. The world is not an entity separate from God but a cloak that both hides and reveals God's presence. Through that cloak, in all its infinite varieties, we can gain a glimpse of the One within. Knowing and loving the universe, whether through understanding the minute organisms studied by the microbiologist or the vast spaces traversed in the mind of the astronomer, is part of our way to knowing and loving God. Torah (or theology) is in this sense a macroscience, a broad framework through which to find meaning in the whole of human endeavor, including the sciences. The mystical religious mind is in no way opposed to science, but rather seeks to encompass it. The *Zohar*'s words, "There is *nothing* that is not referred to in Torah,"[2] should not be taken as a reason to narrow our perspective, limiting study to nothing but Torah itself. Just the opposite, it should mean that Torah is the *broadest* teaching in the universe. All is found within it because all was and is created through it! The laws of physics are Torah, botany and zoology are Torah, and so too is the study of us human creatures and the social forms we have evolved. Thus anthropology, psychology, sociology, and all the rest are to be seen as part of Torah. The internal "secular" nature of these disciplines does not diminish their ultimate religious meaning. All that deepens and enriches our appreciation of God's world is Torah, the roadmap for our journey back to God. It is through the many masks of God that we will come to catch a glimpse of the single "face" that lies behind them all.

The very first Jewish philosopher, Philo of Alexandria, said that Abraham discovered the entire Torah by looking deeply into himself and the world around him. Abraham knew the essential Torah long before it was given, a point also made in the rabbinic tradition. Philo tells us that through contemplation of nature, the patriarch came to understand the natural law, which is one with the law of God. The Hasidic masters were similarly fascinated by the figure of Abraham and discussed the question of what Torah must have been in his day, before the Torah, as we know it, was revealed. This speculation allowed a place for the profound and unitive notion of inner Torah that they were seeking. Rather than insisting that Abraham fulfilled each and every one of the commandments in a literal sense, something that seems quite lacking in the Torah narrative, they claimed that Abraham in an inner or spiritual sense fulfilled all the commandments. The daily acts of piety that he performed contained within them all the *kavvanah,* or spiritual intent, that we possess as we perform our many ritual duties. Here the Hasidic masters follow the beautiful portrait painted by the twelfth-century philosopher Maimonides in the grand concluding chapters of his *Guide to the Perplexed,* in which he depicts the patriarchs as constantly communing with God while they tended their flocks and went about their daily business.[3]

But the later Hasidic masters in Poland went a step further. The *Sefat Emet,* a nineteenth-century Hasidic master, claims that Abraham's deeds *became* Torah, as did the deeds of the other patriarchs and tribes of Israel. The primordial Torah is indeed beyond language; it is nothing but the mysterious name of God, unutterable and beyond comprehension. In order to be received by humans, however, Torah had to be clothed in human deeds. God chose Abraham and his descendents not to be the passive recipients of Torah, but to be those whose lives and actions would be used to embody the hidden Torah as it was to be passed on to future generations. It is because Torah is "made out of all their deeds" that it is accessible to us as well.[4] We humans, in other words, need a human story, a human Torah. Here we see a Judaism that veers very close to what could be called "incarnational" thinking. But the embodiment of Torah is found in the ongoing narrative of Israel as a people, from Abraham through the rebellious tribes of the desert, rather than in the life of a single individual. Judaism is, when all is said and done, the religion of the Jewish people.

This view of Torah helps us to transcend the old struggles surrounding the question of whether Torah is God-given and therefore forever incumbent upon us, or is "merely" a human document and thus can change and evolve over time.[5] Both are true at once. The infinite Torah, the primordial Word of God, echoes through the universe at all times. It is eternal and unchanging. It also cannot be grasped except when clothed in human garments. In our case, these garments are provided by the examples of our ancient heroes, including their human failings, moral struggles, and the personal growth revealed in their stories. So too is the sublime and wordless Torah garbed in the laws and customs of our ancestors, the religious forms and taboos of the written Torah, and later the Oral Torah of tradition, as they were developed and refined over the ages. All of these are human in origin, but they bear within them the divine light of God's Torah and provide us with a pathway by which to journey toward that light. So to the question "Is Torah divine or human?" we can only answer "Yes!"

TORAH REVEALED: THE PLACE OF SINAI

What then do we mean by revelation? Whether we understand the tale of Sinai as a historic event or as a metaphor for the collective religious experience of Israel, we have to ask this question. Here, too, the notion of primordial Torah is the key. Revelation does not necessarily refer to the giving of a truth that we did not possess previously. On the contrary, the primary meaning of revelation means that *our eyes are now opened*, we are able to see that which had been true all along but was hidden from us. We see the same world that existed before the great religious experience, but now we see it differently. The truth that God underlies reality, and always has, now becomes completely apparent.

The Hasidic masters underscore the parallel between the ten commandments revealed at Sinai and the ten utterances of

Creation. The presence of God throughout the world was true from the beginning, but it existed in the form of hidden light, a divine glow that permeates the universe but is accessible only to the great spirits, to seekers as profound as Abraham. At Sinai that light was revealed and made accessible to all. God's "I am," the opening word of the revelation, reverberates through the ages as a "voice that never ceases" (Deut. 5:19), calling forth from Sinai every day, waiting to speak to us today, if only we are here to listen. The ten utterances represent a divine essence of reality that can be discovered by those who seek. Now they are revealed as ten commandments, calling upon *all* of us humans to respond to the divine reality by the way we live.

For the kabbalist these ten utterances are another expression of the ten *sefirot*, the underlying divine structure of all being, which we are soon to study. As with the *sefirot*, these ten are of course one in their essence, not separate from the Oneness of all Being that is God. The Talmud already notes that God says "Let there be" only nine times in the first chapter of Genesis,[6] explaining that "In the beginning" is itself a *ma'amar*, or an utterance of God. That first hidden or preverbal utterance corresponds to *keter*, the highest of the *sefirot*, the place within God (and within religious experience) that remains abstract, elusive, ever beyond our grasp.

What is it that is revealed at Sinai? Revelation is the self-disclosure of God. *Hitgallut*, the Hebrew term for "revelation," is in the reflexive mode, meaning that the gift of Sinai is the gift of God's own self. God has nothing but God to reveal to us. That is why the Rabbis taught that *anokhi*, "I am the Lord your God...," contains every positive commandment in the Torah and "Have no other gods beside Me..." contains all the Torah's prohibitions. The "good news" of Sinai is all there in God's "I am." In response to that eternal truth, we have to learn to be constantly vigilant against our human tendency to make and worship idols.

The Talmud teaches that as God spoke each of the ten words at Sinai, the entire world filled up with a beautiful fragrance. But

then, in an amusing caricature of their own talmudic argumentation, the Rabbis ask: "But if the whole world filled up with fragrance at the first word, the divine "I am," how was there room
for the fragrance of the second word?" "Never mind," is the reply,
"God brought forth a wind from the divine treasure house and
blew it so that the first fragrance would waft away." The word-
ing of this teaching is of special interest. Why did "the whole
world" have to be filled with fragrance as Torah was given? Why
not just the wilderness where Israel stood before the mountain?
This teaching makes it clear that Sinai is a universal event, a
Jewish symbol for all of religious experience, whatever cultural
forms it may take, throughout the world. All humanity has access
to the "fragrance" of Sinai, not just we who stood before that
mountain. It also means that the entire world is *always* filled with
the sweet fragrance of Divine Presence. Just like the voice that
"goes forth from Sinai every day," waiting for the day that we will
be there to hear it, so does the aroma of God's presence ever waft
through the world, seeking us out and hoping that the nasal passages of our spirit will be clear enough for us to catch the smell.

SINAI THEN AND NOW

Revelation, like Creation, is an eternal process. The real
faith–question regarding revelation, like that of Creation, is not
"Do you believe that it happened just that way, so many years
ago?" It is rather, "Are you present to revelation here and now?"
Are our inner ears open to hearing the eternal message that calls
out to us in every moment of existence? That message, the true
essence of revelation, is Torah in its broadest sense, and its call
to us may come through a great variety of channels.

What then of *our* Torah, the concrete document of stories and
commandments, words and letters, that we have before us? The
Torah is our sacred text, the vehicle through which our people receives and pays attention to the eternal Word. Yes, the document

was written by human beings and probably edited from diverse sources over a long period of time. It contains traditions, ways of thinking, and even some limitations that derive from the place and time in which it was written. It also contains some harsh judgments and cruel punishments for Israel's rivals, reflecting the struggle for survival that was our ancestors' lot. There is much in the text that forces us to struggle.

Yet we stand before this Torah in a way that reaches beyond its surface meanings. Torah is the text that reveals to us the name and reality of God. It is the book of "I am Y-H-W-H" and of "I shall be what I shall be." We read the text with an openness that allows us to discover that presence within it. It may be in the words, in the mystery of the letters, or in the silent spaces that lie between them. Hearing the Torah read in the synagogue itself becomes an exercise in deep listening, a way of letting ourselves hear that which usually eludes us. In doing so, we open our hearts to be *commanded*, to stand as at Sinai and to receive the Word. In that moment the ten utterances of Creation are transformed into the imperative voice and become the ten words, or commandments, of Sinai. All the other commandments of Torah, we are told, are present in these and derive from them. Sinai changes nothing, only revealing to us that which had been true all along. It also changes everything. As the ten divine utterances make that shift from the declarative to the imperative mode, Torah makes its claim on us, its demand that we shape our lives, as individuals and as a community, in *response* to that revelation.

This moment of receiving, hearing, and accepting Torah is one we share with all Israel, everywhere, across space and time. Yes, Torah is heard differently in each generation, as the Hasidic masters knew well. But we are still challenged to respond to it. We will speak later of prayer as a way of "giving" oneself as a response to the gift of God's presence. But especially characteristic of Judaism is the way of responding by means of study and interpretation. We receive Torah as raw material, an ancient, rough-hewn teaching that we believe contains locked within it the memory of a deep encounter with God—*our* deep encounter with God. But how do we unlock its secrets?

The Rabbis understood this long ago, when they compared Torah to a gift of flax, given by a king to two servants before he set out on a journey. "Who is the faithful servant?" asks the midrash. "The one who has a bag of flax to give to the king upon his return, or the one who has woven that flax into a beautiful garment?"[7]

How do we go about weaving that garment for our time? The answer for us is no different than it was for any other generation: by living and learning, learning and living. To paraphrase the German-Jewish philosopher Franz Rosenzweig, I believe that we have to go both "from Torah to life"—letting Torah guide us as to the proper way to live—and "from life to Torah," creating new Torah based on our own life experience. This book is an attempt to move in both of those directions.

We are ready now to turn to the first of these tasks, learning the language of Kabbalah and applying it in a contemporary way. We begin with ancient tradition and apply it to our own inner lives. We will do this with regard to *sefirot* (the "stages" in the inner divine life), *'olamot* (the "worlds" of kabbalistic reality), and *shemot* (the names of God). Afterwards we will turn to our own world to address the kind of religious teaching called for by our times and the lives we lead.

4

Sefirot: The One and the Ten

WHAT DO WE MEAN?

*E*YN SOF, GOD AS ENDLESS, LIMITLESS, undifferentiated reality, is the beginning and the end of truth. Everything else happens in between. The oneness of *Eyn Sof* is absolute; it is a "One" that does not begin a series of numbers, a One so total that no "two" can possibly come after it. A "One" that includes all that ever was, is, and will be cannot be followed by a "two." Even if there can be no "two," say the kabbalists, there can be a "ten." The One opens up to reveal itself as ten. The ten *sefirot* ("numbers," or stages) within the cosmic structure are not *added* to *Eyn Sof*, but are revealed as existing within it, the reward of a deeper gaze into reality and its nature. Using our Arabic (actually Indian-derived) numerals, we may say that "10" adds nothing but a zero to the "1," but opens it to a deeper dimension. These stages are described in most kabbalistic sources as the primal process, the steps by which the hidden mystery becomes the God of the Torah, the Creator and Revealer, the God of history and redemption.

The contemporary Jewish mystic has to be somewhat more modest in the claims made for the "truth" of the sefirotic model.

To say that I know how God emerges from the depths of mystery and sets out to create the world is far more than I would dare to assert in an "objective" way. The important thing for today's seeker is to begin from experience, not from metaphysics. What the kabbalist *does* know is how he or she emerges from those depths of mystery, returning from an experience of unity and loss of self, and reestablishes a firm grounding in the realm of ordinary consciousness. The *sefirot* are stages of spiritual "ascent," going up the ladder of abstraction until one is fully lost or absorbed in the mystery of Oneness. They are also rungs of "descent," the return to this "lower" world of daily reality. Kabbalah claims that this path, one we can come to know through contemplative practice and whose truth is validated by inner experience, is the cosmic path, and that our experience is only a recapitulation of God's own way into the world.

The *sefirot* may also be seen on an outer/inner axis rather than a vertical one, a model that will work better for some in our day. We make the journey *inward* toward Oneness, to a *deeper* level of being, and return from it through the same ten stages, to the external, or outer reality, of daily living. So too does God emerge out of the inner, hidden depths to manifest in the unique surface form of each and every creature. It is *a statement of faith, not a recital of fact* that the kabbalist sees this inner process as recapitulating the origins of the cosmos itself. The human mind is a microcosm, a miniature replica of the Divine. Each human being is the image of God. To the kabbalist this means that by turning inward, contemplating the inner stages by which the self emerges, we may gain some insight about the cosmic Self as well.

FIRST TRIAD: THE PRIMAL PROCESS

Keter

Keter represents the first stirrings of intent within *Eyn Sof,* the arousal of desire to come forth into the varied life of being. To

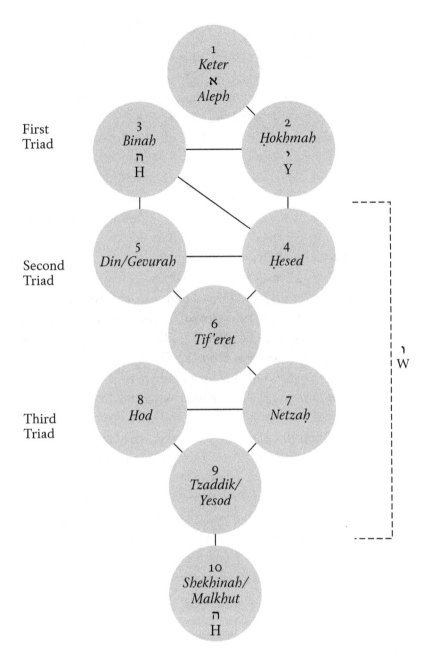

The Ten *Sefirot*

say it in the language of experience, it is the first wholly unde-
fined awakening of an urge toward movement within the detached and abstracted self. There is no specific "content" in *keter;*
it is a desire that potentially bears all content, but actually none.
It is therefore often designated by the kabbalists as "Nothing." All
beings (and all mystic voyagers) must traverse this realm of
Nothingness, this transit stage between being wholly within the
One and the first glimmer of separate existence. Indeed, some
Hasidic masters taught that the journey to and from the Nothing
is continual, the greatest constant of existence.

While *keter* is still devoid of content, it is already identified
as a locus of pure compassion. Here we recall our earlier discussion of *keter* as *Ehyeh.* In its very emptiness, *keter* accepts and wel-
comes the future, turning with compassion toward all that is to
be. We might refer to it as a state of divine openness. *Keter* is the
starting-point of the cosmic process. The word *keter* means
"crown," and this rung of being is sometimes referred to as *keter
'elyon,* the Supreme Crown of God. This image is derived from a
depiction of the ten *sefirot* in anthropic form, that is to say, in the
image of a human being. This image is adapted from an ancient
myth that saw God crowned each day by the prayers of Israel.[1] As
this personification is of a royal personage, the highest manifestation of this emerging spiritual "body" will be the crown.

But the more primary meaning of the word *keter* is "circle"; it is
from this that the notion of the crown is derived. The most ancient
document that speaks of *sefirot* is *Sefer Yetsirah,* the *Book of Creation.*
There we are told that the *sefirot* are a great circle, "their end tied to
their beginning, their beginning to their end." The circularity of the
sefirot will be important to us as we go further in our description.

Ḥokhmah

Out of *keter* emerges *ḥokhmah,* or "Wisdom," the first and finest
point of "real" existence. All things, souls, and moments of time

that are ever to be, now exist within a primal point, at once infinitesimally small and great beyond measure. (Like mystics everywhere, kabbalists love the language of paradox, a way of showing how inadequate words really are to describe this reality.) The move from *keter* to *ḥokhmah*, the first step in the primal process, is a transition from Nothingness to being, from pure potential to the first point of real existence. The kabbalists are fond of describing it by their own reading of Job 28:12, the opening verse of Job's hymn to Wisdom: "Wisdom comes from Nothingness." All the variety of existence is contained within *ḥokhmah*, ready to begin the journey forward. The primal point contains within it the potential of all that is to be.

Ḥokhmah is also the primordial teaching, the inner mind of God, the Torah that exists prior to the birth of words and letters. As Being exists first in this ultimately concentrated form, so too does truth or wisdom. Here we begin to see the kabbalists' insistence that Creation and Revelation are twin processes, existence and language, the real and the nominal, emerging together from the hidden mind of God. As the primal point of existence, *ḥokhmah* is symbolized by the letter *yod*, the smallest of the letters, the first point from which all other letters will be written. All of Torah, the text and the commentary added to it in every generation—indeed, all of human wisdom—is contained within a single *yod*. This *yod*—written ׳, is the first letter of the name of God. The upper tip of the *yod* is said to point toward *keter*, itself designated by the *aleph* or the divine name *Ehyeh*.

Binah

This journey from inner divine Nothingness toward the beginning of existence is one that inevitably arouses duality, even within the inner realms. As *ḥokhmah* emerges, it brings forth its own mate, called *binah*, or "Contemplation." These two may be experienced within the self as two aspects of mind: *ḥokhmah*, the first flash of intellect, the creative spark, and *binah,* the depth of thought that then absorbs the spark, shaping and refining it as it takes it into itself. Ḥokhmah is described as a point of light that seeks out a grand mirrored palace of reflection. The light seen back and forth in those countless mirrored surfaces is all one light, but infinitely transformed and magnified in the reflective process.

Ḥokhmah and *binah* are inseparably linked; either one is inconceivable to us without the other. Ḥokhmah is too fine and subtle to be detected without its reflections or reverberations in *binah.* The mirrored halls of *binah* would be dark and unknowable without the light of *ḥokhmah.* For this reason these two are often treated by kabbalists as the primal pair, ancestral *Abba* and *Imma,* Father and Mother, deepest polarities of male and female within the divine (and human) Self. The point and the palace are thus also primal Male and Female, each transformed and fulfilled in their union with one another. The energy that radiates from the point of *ḥokhmah* is described chiefly in metaphors of flowing light and water, verbal pictures used by the mystics to speak of these most abstract levels of the inner mind. But images of sexual union are never far behind these. Ḥokhmah's flow of light is also the flow of seed. Ḥokhmah is filled to the bursting point with the potential energy of all that is to be; it fills the womb of *binah* and "she" gives birth to all the further rungs within the ten-in-one divine structure, the seven lower *sefirot.*

A GUIDED MEDITATION

This might be a good place to pause for a period of meditation, a time to absorb this teaching in an experiential way. Laying out the path of *sefirot* in sequence bears the danger of just imparting *information,* and that is precisely what the *sefirot* are not. We are talking here about inner stages of the mind's reality that should correspond to something within our own experience. Let us try, then, to appreciate this language in the form of a guided meditation.

Prepare yourself by becoming still, seated or standing in a comfortable position and in a quiet, undisturbed place. Begin by following your rhythmic breathing for a few minutes, allowing thoughts to pass by you, keeping the mind as empty and free as you are able. Then turn your mind to contemplation.

Binah, *endless breadth of spirit, mind expanded and relaxed in cool contemplation. Allow the spirit to expand beyond its limits as you open to the broadest inner places. Out of all narrowness, beyond all constraints. To go to* binah, *release yourself from the pull of emotions and powerful feelings of any sort. All desire, even the desire to understand, should be left behind in turning alone to this place of inner mind.* Binah, *called "thought" or "pure mind," contemplates nothing that is not itself. Enter into that chamber of pure contemplation, mind embracing mind itself.*

Binah *is also the womb of God as Great Mother, the Source of life to which all life longs to return.* Teshuvah, *or "return to God," is another name for* binah. *In* binah *we go back to our deepest source, our most ancient memory. Beyond words or language, we release ourselves to float freely in this deep pool of contemplation. We have returned to the womb of Being, the place out of which our soul was drawn. But now we recall the old rabbinic legend that before our birth a candle was lighted within the womb, and by its light we studied the Torah we would need before going forth into the world of lies. Here, too, we see the candle burning at the center of the pool. Approach that flame, allowing yourself to be drawn to it, then absorbed by it. Fire in water, the vision of paradox. The light of* hokhmah *becomes the new focus of the dissolved, contemplative self. "In Your light we see light," says the psalmist. This is the first and final light, the source of truth that guides us in the highest stage of our journey to and from non-being.*

SECOND TRIAD: SEEKING INNER BALANCE

Out of the womb of *binah* flow the seven "lower" *sefirot,* the seven aspects of the divine Self. Together, these seven constitute the God who is the subject of worship and the One whose image is reflected in each human soul. The divine persona, as conceived by Kabbalah, is an interplay of these seven forces or inner directions. So too is each human personality, God's image in the world. The Hasidic masters make much of this psychological aspect of Kabbalah's teachings. This "holy structure" of the inner life of God is the essential secret of all Jewish mysticism, it is the "Mystery of Faith," as described in magnificently poetic form by the *Zohar* and as refined in countless images by kabbalists through the ages. "God," in other words, is the first Being to emerge out of the divine womb, the primal entity to take shape as the endless energies of *Eyn Sof* begin to coalesce.

Although in human life we experience the *sefirot* as existing simultaneously with one another, each responding to and balancing the potential excesses of another, the kabbalists traditionally describe them in sequence, as they emerge from the primal process we have just described. Again, this sequence does not have to be linear, as the *sefirot* exist within the timeless Self of Y-H-W-H. The sequence is rather one of intrinsic logic, each stage responding to that which comes "before" it. The structure consists of two dialectical triads (sets of thesis, antithesis, and synthesis) and a final vehicle of reception that also energizes the entire system from "below," corresponding to *keter* at the "upper" end. These are the stages of the inner life of God, known to us through their reflection in the human psyche, especially seen in the process of journeys to and from the experience of inward union.

Ḥesed and Gevurah

First to manifest is *ḥesed,* the grace or love of God. The emergence of God from hiding is an act filled with love, a promise of an endless showering of blessing and life on all beings, each of whom will continue this process of emerging from the One. This gift of love is beyond measure and without limit. The boundless compassion of *keter* is now transposed into a love for each specific form and creature that is ever to emerge. This channel of grace is the original divine *shefa'*, the bounteous love of God of which the psalmist says, "His mercies are over all His work" (Ps. 145:9). As we emerge from Oneness, we too are filled with love for each and every creature.

But the divine wisdom also understands that love alone is not the way to bring forth "other" beings and allow them their place. Love unbounded can be so powerful that it overwhelms the other, never allowing it to leave the first embrace and set forth on its own journey. *Ḥesed* therefore emerges linked to its own opposite, described both as *din*, the judgment of God, and as *gevurah*, the bastion of divine power. This is a force that measures and limits love, controlling the flow of *ḥesed* in accord with the needs, abilities, and deserts of those who are to receive it.

Ḥesed is the God of love, calling forth in us the response of love. *Ḥesed* in the soul is our love of God and all of God's creatures, our ability to continue this divine flow, passing on to others the gift of love. *Gevurah* represents the God we fear, the One before whose power we stand in trembling. Rather than personifying a childish fear, the cringing of a guilty youngster before a punishing parent, *gevurah* represents our awe before the majesty and magnificence of the cosmos, the smallness we feel as we open ourselves to the totality of Being. Here we are reminded of our own mortality and limited strength, as we contemplate the endless power of the One compared to the briefness of each human life. It is no wonder that the kabbalists see *ḥesed* as the faith of Abraham, described by the prophet as "Abraham who loves Me." As *ḥesed* is first to emerge within God, Abraham is the first of God's earthly followers, the man of love, the one who will leave everything behind and follow God across the deserts. He offers

EHYEH
Mind Beyond Mind
Pure Compassion
The Ancient One
First Ripple in
Stillness of *Eyn Sof*
Uppermost Crown

Palace of Reflection
Contemplation
Womb of Existence
Teshuvah–Return to
the Deepest Source
Spring
First Temple

Primal Point
Spark of Existence
Hidden Torah
Deep Well
Hidden "Father" of
All Being

Power, Judgment
Measuring of
Divine Love
Left Hand
Isaac
North
Obedience, Discipline

Grace
Free-flowing Love
of God
Right Hand
Abraham
South
Generosity, Openheartedness

The Blessed Holy One
Glory, Truth
Jacob/Israel
Male Torso
East/Rising Sun
Balance, Harmony
Perfect Center

Beauty
Aaron
Left Thigh
Gratitude, Acceptance

Triumph, Victory
Moses
Right Thigh
Self-Confidence, Dream
of Perfection
Messianic Vision

Rivers,
Channels
of Flow

Rectifier
Foundation
Joseph
Phallus/Covenant
Balance Restored
Stable Personality

Indwelling Presence
God's Kingdom/Community of Israel
David/Rachel
Tabernacle/Ark
Jerusalem/Western Wall
Sea, Moon
Bride of God; Mother of Lower Worlds
Female Complement
Lower Crown

Key Symbols of the Ten *Sefirot*

to God the gift of his entire life; he is even willing to place his beloved son upon the altar. *Gevurah,* on the other hand, represents the God called "fear of Isaac." This is the divine face Isaac sees when bound to that altar, confronting the God he believes is about to demand his life. Isaac's piety is of a different quality than his father's. Trembling obedience, rather than love, marks his path through life.

The linking together of *ḥesed* and *gevurah* is an infinitely delicate balance. Too much love and the other has no room to exist. Isaac will indeed die because of Abraham's unbounded love. But too much power or judgment is even worse. The kabbalists see this *gevurah* aspect of both the divine and human self as fraught with danger, the very birthplace of evil. The *Zohar* tells of a discontent on this "left," or *gevurah,* side of God. *Gevurah* becomes impatient with *ḥesed,* unhappy with its endless casting aside of judgment in the name of love. Our judging side grows weary with love, wanting to get on with the punishment that the "other" (most often another part of our own self) so clearly deserves. Rather than doing its job of permitting love to flow in measured ways, *gevurah* seeks out a cosmic moment to rule alone, to hold back the flow of love. In this moment divine power turns to rage or fury; out of it all the forces of evil are born, darkness emerges from the light of God, a shadow of the divine universe that is also manifest in each of us as our ability to do evil.

Here we have one of the most important moral lessons of Kabbalah. Judgment untempered by love brings about evil; power obsessed with itself turns demonic. Evil is not some distant force. It resides within each of us, as it exists in the cosmos as a whole, the result of an imbalance of inner forces. Neither the world nor the self can do without *gevurah,* represented in the person by self-restraint, strength of character, and the knowledge of how to act appropriately in any given situation. We constantly must ensure, though, that enough love and compassion break through these restraints or else we are in grave danger of harming ourselves and those around us, upsetting the balance of our own inner lives. Anger, in particular, is frowned upon by the kabbalistic ethos, which always wants us to lean toward the "right," or *ḥesed,* side of the self, making sure that our love remains strong and is free to flow.

Tif'eret

The balance of *ḥesed* and *gevurah* is called *tif'eret,* or "splendor," by the kabbalists. This perfectly poised Being is the God before whom we stand in prayer and the One whose person is ideally mirrored in our own lives. Sometimes this rung is referred to as *emet,* or "truth." The three Hebrew letters of *emet*—אמת—represent the first, middle, and last letters of the alphabet. Truth is stretched forth across the whole of Being, joining the extremes of right and left, *ḥesed* and *gevurah,* into a single integrated personality. This ideal figure is represented by the third patriarch, Jacob, also called Israel, the perfect integration of the forces of Abraham and Isaac. This is not the Jacob of biblical stories, depicted as having a somewhat questionable moral character. The kabbalist's Jacob is the idealized patriarch, "the elder Israel" (Jacob's new name gained in his struggle with the angel) of the rabbinic imagination, the source of blessing for all of his children and all who later identify as "the children of Israel."

In Jacob, or *tif'eret,* we reach the synthesis that resolves the original tension between *ḥesed* and *gevurah,* the inner right and left, love and judgment. The "we" refers to each human being, because what we have here is a model of human personality. Jacob, in this sense, is the perfect human—a new Adam, according to the sages—the radiant-faced elder extending blessing through the world. The "we" also includes God, according to the kabbalists, for we humans are the mirror-image of the God we worship. This God knows us because our struggle to integrate love and judgment is not ours alone, but the reflection of a cosmic struggle. The inner structure of our psychic life is the hidden structure of the universe; it is because of this that we can come to know God by the path of inward contemplation and true self-knowledge.

A POST-MODERN DIGRESSION

On this point a difference does and does not exist (paradox again!) between the pre-modern and the post-modern kabbalist. To us post-moderns, it may seem clear that what we are describing here is projection: "God" is structured this way because this image of God is the creation of humans, and, in fact, the creation of Jews, and this is the way we have conceived our God. The essential tension between love and judgment is part of human experience, reflecting our struggles in relating both to ourselves and to others. In particular, this struggle is very much that of the Rabbis, who love both the people and the Law. Trained toward kindliness and compassion, they are also the upholders of tradition, and they often find themselves having to choose between the love of Israel and the love of Torah. The love of Israel leads them toward compassion and leniency, while loving and defending the law leads them to lean toward the side of judgment. This tension runs deeply through the rabbinic tradition and is reflected in the Rabbis' projected image of a God who struggles between love and justice.

Some voices within the kabbalistic tradition would agree that all of our images of God are, in fact, projection. "A figure with the appearance of a man" is on the great chariot-throne of Ezekiel's vision, according to the Hasidic rabbi of Apt, because we place Him there.[2] In fact, we are required to do so; God demands of us that we create the projection of God that we can worship! The God who is the source of that demand must therefore be a God beyond all images. The Endless One or source of all, present within us as within all that is, manifests itself to us in a way that calls upon us to create religions, worshipful forms in which we can acknowledge that One. This includes fashioning images of the Divine that make the mystery accessible to us, both intellectually and emotionally. God as Father as well as Mother, God as kindly Ruler and passionate Lover—also God as flowing stream and shining light—are all part of this great human effort to give word and image to that which lies beyond expression in either.

In short, we may accept from modernity the psychological and historical insights that view religion as projection. But our post-modernity requires us to go another step, this one learned from the insights of mystics in our tradition as well as others. The mirror of projection goes both ways. We may project a God-image that reflects us, but God may also project a human image that reflects God. We may have projected a God who reflects our own cultural and historical setting, but we did so because we felt within us the stirring of a deeper reality in which we ourselves are mere projections. The human brain conceives of a Cosmic Mind of which the brain itself is a tiny copy. Or does the Cosmic Mind, the "mainframe" of intellect in the universe, replicate itself in some miniscule way in that mini-wonder called the human brain? Who can determine where this hall of mirrors begins? It seems hardly likely that it begins with us alone. "The eye with which I see God and the eye with which God sees me are the same eye," says the great Christian mystic Meister Eckhardt. The mirror turns both ways.

THIRD TRIAD: STRIVING AND ACCEPTANCE

Netzaḥ and Hod

Our inner Jacob, the figure of perfect balance, can also be one of pride. In fact, the term tif'eret, which we rendered as "splendor," denotes something very close to pride. "I have resolved the great conflict. Here I stand, in perfect balance: loving, generous, but still able to judge." Now the balanced, centered figure of Jacob leans too far toward the right, and synthesis becomes the new thesis, the unbalanced, extreme view. *Tif'eret* gives rise to *netzaḥ,* or "triumph." The *netzaḥ* in our personality celebrates our victory and believes that we can be triumphant over all enemies of perfection, whatever they may be. Now that we have subdued anger and allowed love to flow in ways that nourish and do not destroy, wholeness itself seems within our grasp. This is the flaw within *tif'eret,* that which sets up a second tension, a new level of dialectical strain within the self. An inner sense of perfect balance can lead to the danger of triumphalism: "I have won the great battle. I can do it all; nothing will stand in my way."

The *netzaḥ* within us needs and calls forth a new opposing force called *hod. Hod* means "beauty," but some connect it also to *hodayah,* which means both "gratitude" and "confession" or "admission." *Netzaḥ* seeks to remake the world, to render everything perfect. It is a great force for goodness, that which inspires us to go forth and right the world's wrongs, to reform the social order, to fulfill the dream of perfection. *Hod* is the admission that we cannot do it all, the acknowledgment that we have to accept ourselves as we are and be grateful for life as it has been given to us. Beauty lies in that which is, if only we open our inner eye to behold it. *Netzaḥ* strives for transformation; it is the impatient force within us that believes we can accomplish anything, that reality should be subject to our wise reshaping power. *Hod* is the other side of wisdom, the self that bows before the mystery of what is *as* it is, the self who submits to reality and rejoices in doing so.

The biblical figures represented by *netzaḥ* and *hod* are Moses and Aaron. Moses is the outer form of the inner Jacob, according to the kabbalists. We may see it as perfection that takes on the challenge of leadership. The Moses within us stares down Pharaoh, the embodiment of evil and oppression. That Moses leads our forces out of Egypt, parting the sea with the staff of confidence placed in his hand, but our inner troops get weary and start to lose their way. Confident that we can pull it all together, that we can make it all the way to the Promised Land, we lead on. In the struggle for victory and transformation, however, we lose some of our patience. Exasperated with our own inability to do it all, we follow Moses in arguing both with his God and his people.

Here we need the wisdom of Aaron the priest. Bowing deeply before the altar, he knows how to accept reality as it is. Even when tragedy befalls him—Aaron lost two sons to an excess of religious enthusiasm—he stands silent in acceptance, knowing he will continue in the life of worship. Perhaps life cannot be changed; Aaron accepts it and finds it beautiful as it is. He even accepts and understands the needs of those who demand a Golden Calf. Devotion, gratitude, acceptance: these are the virtues of our inner high priest.

Tzaddik (Yesod)

The synthesis of *netzaḥ* and *hod*, Moses and Aaron, transforming prophet and accepting priest, is *tzaddik*, the Righteous One who lives within us. This is Joseph, the son and direct successor of Jacob, now refined by resolving this new struggle between transformation and acceptance. The ninth *sefirah*, the synthesis of the second inner struggle, is *tzaddik* in a sense that I would here translate as "rectifier," that one who rectifies or sets straight the course. This redirected, straightened course has been through the excess zeal of *netzaḥ*, often exemplified by youth, in which everything is going to be made perfect. Tempered by the wisdom and appreciativeness of *hod*, it is ready to become the foundation (*yesod* in Hebrew, a frequently found name for this rung) of stable personality. This stage represents a new fullness or maturity of personal development. It is the balanced self after another round of testing, the one who knows where to strive and where to accept limits. It represents *shalom*, the wholeness of inner peace.

In theory this synthesis, too, could become a new thesis, calling forth yet another opposite and another resolution, and so on *ad infinitum.* The dialectic is an unending process. So too is the task of inner growth, the challenging and refining of human personality. But the point has already been made, and once is enough. A tenfold model has a simple perfection about it that would be lost if we were to carry it further. The first nine *sefirot* thus represent three triads, one describing the primal process out of which personhood, both divine and human, is born; followed by the two triads of tension and resolution, taking us to the place of peace. Life-energy is endlessly coursing through this pattern, binding the *sefirot* together into a single whole. This is the energy that will flow from God into the world, allowing all creatures to exist as varied manifestations of the single One. Before the border can be crossed from Oneness into multiplicity, however, that energy must be received into the great and transformative storehouse of Being, represented by the final link in the inner divine process, God as *shekhinah,* or abundant Presence.

THE TENTH *SEFIRAH:* PROCESS FULFILLED

Shekhinah (Malkhut)

The word *shekhinah* derives from the Hebrew root שכן meaning "to dwell." One noun formed from that root is *mishkan,* the tabernacle or dwelling place of God in the wilderness. *Mishkan* means "the place of dwelling;" *shekhinah* is more like "that which dwells." *Shekhinah* is the presence of the One amid the many, the palpable reality of divinity within the here-and-now. The first nine *sefirot* refer to a reality that transcends our ordinary life experience. They represent the transition or the inner journey from hiddenness to manifestation, from *Eyn Sof* to *shekhinah,* in both God and person. The final *sefirah,* especially as understood in the Hasidic sources, is the God who is fully immanent within the natural and physical world, the God who is the subject of our regular awareness that "the whole earth is filled with God's glory."

The imagery associated with *shekhinah* in kabbalistic teaching is particularly rich. She is *malkhut,* the "kingdom" into which the King enters and in which perfect harmony and fulfillment are found. Most of the verbal images portray *shekhinah* in feminine terms or in aspects of nature, such as land, sea, and moon, natural elements that are often linked to femininity. This has to do with the deeply sexual character of kabbalistic thought. The flow of energy or being through the sefirotic channels, while sometimes likened to both light and water flowing from a hidden source, is very much experienced by the kabbalist as the flow of a man's inner sexual energies, concentrated in the semen that he pours into his mate at the moment of sexual climax. Kabbalah rejects the usual Western separation of the physical from the spiritual realm. The flow of divinity from hiddenness to revelation, the flow of mental energies from egolessness to fullness of personality, and the flow of sexual energies from their deep inner sources to fulfillment in the act of sexual union are all manifestations of the same process.

The kabbalists, like people of all ages, were filled with wonder at the human reproductive process. Their teachings are in part a reflection on the links between love, its passionate fulfillment, and the flow of creative energies throughout the universe. The connection between our words *creation* and *procreation* derives from this same perception of reality. The forces within our human make-up that lead us to bring forth new generations lie in a continuum with the power that brought us here in the first place. Thus the human soul and even the existence of the lower worlds altogether are depicted by Kabbalah as resulting from an act of sexual union within God, of the flow together of divine male and female energies.

The Kabbalah of previous centuries was created, transmitted, taught, and studied exclusively by men. Books written for women, usually in the vernacular rather than Hebrew, were notably devoid of kabbalistic teachings. It is thus no surprise that the sexual model offered by Kabbalah is designed entirely from a male point of view. The "upper" six of the seven *sefirot* that constitute divine and human personhood are usually seen as male; only the seventh, the receptive partner, is female. *Shekhinah* is like the moon, having no light of her own, waiting to receive the light of the sun as it shines forth upon her. She is the sea, into whom the waters flow; the holy city, entered by the holy King. *Shekhinah* is the bride of God, longing for her husband to join her under the canopy that represents their love. She also represents the exiled Community of Israel, who longs for her absent spouse to return to her and restore her former glory.

Shekhinah is not without significant power, however. It is she who must begin the arousal of love. Energized by the devotion of her followers, she turns to arouse her divine Lover and awaken the flow from beyond. Energy thus courses in both directions: forward through the sefirotic channels and into *shekhinah,* but also back from the outer world, into *shekhinah* and up through the *sefirot,* reaching back toward *keter.* The *sefirot* may be seen in the image of Jacob's dream, a ladder reaching from earth to heaven, with angels going up and down on it. *Shekhinah* is the ground on which the ladder stands; it is she who sends the angels upward. The *Zohar* compares *shekhinah* to the holy Sabbath, a day on which no manna fell in the wilderness and when no productive work is allowed, but the day that is the source of blessing for all the others. Were it not for the blessings sent forth by *shekhinah,* the life-force flowing through the upper channels could never come to fruition.

A Kabbalah for our times, taught and studied by women as well as men, will need to develop new and more nuanced understandings of this inner union from a female as well as a male perspective. As a male teacher of Kabbalah, I would not presume to say what form this development will take. It may portray female understandings of all the *sefirot* or it may open *shekhinah* herself to multiple levels of discovery and understanding. The growth of these teachings will require time, patience, much knowledge, and true inspiration. These teachings cannot be artificial or seem superficially imposed. If they are deeply rooted in the traditions of the past and remain faithful to the essential values of uniting all and revealing the One manifest in both male and female, I trust that they will eventually be accepted.

COMPLETING THE CIRCLE

As we conclude our discussion of the ten *sefirot*, we need to talk about the special relationship between the first and the last of the ten. One of the most important names for *shekhinah* in Kabbalah is *'atarah*, another Hebrew term for "crown." The first and last

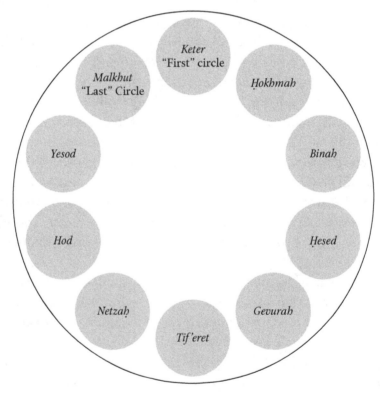

Sefirot as the Circle of Existence

sefirot are both crowns, *keter* and *'atarah*. We said above that the word *keter* also means "circle," because the crown is round. Now we should see the *sefirot* as a sacred circle, "its end tied to its beginning and its beginning to its end," as the ancient *Sefer Yetzirah* teaches. The ten *sefirot* as a circle represent the fullness of God, the complete circle, the Oneness of Being. Because *shekhinah* dwells within us and we within it, we, too, are part of that circle. The circle of life includes all that is. In order to understand the process, to trace the origins of the many back to the One, we have allowed ourselves to open that circle, to turn it temporarily into a series of straight lines, so that we might see its progression, going from one stage to another. This is the way our linear minds work; it is the style of what we sometimes call right-brain thinking. Now that we have come to the end of the system, we must remember, as the kabbalists are quick to remind us, that really we understand nothing at all. Therefore we rejoin the circle, tie its ends back together, and allow ourselves to dance within it.

Here again, we are ready for a meditation. The ten *sefirot* must become a way of thinking for us, not a body of knowledge. They are the choreography for a dance of the mind, to be apprehended always by the left side of the brain, that which appreciates poetry and hears its inner music. Let us try to contemplate the *sefirot* in a kind of poetic framework.

> *Nothing is at the beginning.*
> *Nothing is at the end.*
> *Let me be a vessel,*
> *Drawing together*
> *One with One,*
> *So they become One in my hands,*
> *So that we become one in Your hands.*
> *One within, One beyond;*
> *One above, One below;*
> *One right, One left;*
> *One he, One she;*

One I, one Thou.
Ten in One,
One in Ten
Present here,
Present now.
All is at the beginning.
All is at the end.

5

'Olamot: Four Steps to Oneness

NAMING THE "WORLDS"

T HE TEN *SEFIROT* are seen by the kabbalist as the inner structure of all reality. Both the macrocosm, or the universe, and
the microcosm, the individual human mind, are fashioned according to this structure. Overlaid on this grid of ten *sefirot* many
kabbalists also speak of four *'olamot* (literally, "worlds"), or levels of spiritual awareness. These four worlds, in ascending order,
are named for three biblical terms for Creation and the Hebrew
word for emanation, or the flow of inner energy. From a psychological point of view, they trace the individual's evolving understanding of God. As such, they may become essential tools for
our own contemporary search.

The first or "lowest" of these "worlds" is called *'asiyah* (literally, "doing" or "activity"). This is the realm of separate identity,
the inner place where we live most of our lives, where ego-identity
dominates and makes our perception of reality begin with our
identity as distinct, separate selves. "I think, therefore I am." The
very fact of mind, on the *'asiyah* level, reinforces ego identity. The
self of *'asiyah* is not necessarily a selfish or a materialistic self; it

is possible to lead a good life while remaining on the 'asiyah plane. It is a world, however, that remains far from mystical insight, one in which the duality of Creator and creature and the reality of individual identity stand completely unchallenged.

One stage beyond this is *yetsirah* (literally, "formation"), the world where separateness begins to slip away as we join into the chorus of the angels, recognizing that there are higher forms of life (or "deeper rungs of perception") of which we are also a part. These rungs are many, even infinite, in number. As we remove the blinders of 'asiyah that limited us to a single sort of consciousness, we begin to understand that rung after rung opens to a deeper and truer way of perceiving reality. Thus we begin to climb the inward ladder, finding that we do not have to *experience* all of the rungs or stages to know that they exist; each insight brings with it the renewed awareness of how many more lie beyond it.

In the third stage, *beri'ah* (literally, "creation"), we see the great vision. The magnificence of divine truth is now laid out before us. We understand that there is only one reality. The multiplicity of rungs is left behind, melting before the grandeur of this insight: There is only One; that One is God in the heavens "above" and on the earth "beneath." All the many rungs of being are but one; "there is nothing else." Still, in this *beri'ah* consciousness, *I* am somehow still here as the one who has been granted that insight. The mind is close to bursting with the fullness of the vision, but it is still the mind. Referring back to the Ba'al Shem Tov's parable of the king and the illusory palace, at this stage I might know that "there is nothing there but the King," but it is still "I" who have that insight.

The final stage leads beyond. No longer describable in the language of Creator and Creation, it is called *atsilut*, or "flowing." Here the lines between self and Self no longer exist; macrocosmic universe and microcosmic mind are a pair of mirrors that stand opposite each other; they reflect one another so fully that any attempt to distinguish between them has to be left behind. In *atsilut* there is nothing other than the flow.

In this chapter I will offer my own approach to these stages of spiritual development. We will use a series of traditional images of the God/human relationship as depicted in Jewish sources to help you appreciate and experience inner growth in the religious imagination. The journey through the *'olamot* is seen here as a paradigm for stages in the life of faith as I have come to know them. The association between these images and the four worlds is my way of sharing with you something of my own journey from "world" to "world." Once again, I hope that it might reflect and cast light on some aspects of your journey as well.

'ASIYAH: GOD AS KING

The God of *'asiyah* is God as King. *'Asiyah* is the place of the fear of God. In Hebrew this is called *yir'ah* or *yir'at ha-shem*, "the fear of the Lord." Because ego is strong when we are in *'asiyah* consciousness, we confront God as a Being outside ourselves, a transcendent Other who has power infinitely greater than our own. God as the object of *yir'ah* is usually depicted as God the King. (I could say "Ruler" or "Sovereign," but here I believe that the maleness of the image is part of its power.) The great Creator has put us into this world, given us the gift of an instant of life within the vast stretch of eternity, and called upon each of us to respond by creating something of value with it. The privilege of living is great, but the demand is overwhelming, fearsome. The King is the One who confronts us and addresses us with that demand.

The royal metaphor for God is an ancient one, stretching back into long-forgotten antiquity. Israel adopted it from the Near Eastern culture out of which it emerged. In other parts of the world, too, as societies came to evolve into kingdoms, kings began to assert divine authority and the gods began to be described as kings. It seemed natural to the ancients that the all-powerful

Creator should be spoken of in the language of kingship, with humans as loyal subjects. Eventually the one God came to be known as the "King of kings," meaning that God's rule surpassed that of mere earthly monarchs.

While such a way of speaking may seem distant in our age, the mythic power of this royal language is still very great. To begin the spiritual journey with *yir'ah* and divine kingship is to acknowledge a power beyond the self. Submission plays a vital role in the growth of spiritual awareness. As long as we are dominated by the ego's endless cycles of pride and insecurity, we will not achieve inner peace. *Yir'ah* should not come to intimidate us, but to help us accept our own limitations and to see ourselves as living within a universe greater than ourselves, but one in which we have a proper place.

Yir'ah is also awe, a sense of trembling before the greatness of God, as described in the Torah's description of Mount Sinai: "All the people, seeing the thunderbolts and torches and hearing the *shofar* sounding as the mountain smoked—the people were frightened; they trembled and stood far off" (Ex. 20:14). In the consciousness of *'asiyah* we must stand at some distance from God. We are not ready to come closer; to do so would run the risk that we take God's presence for granted. This, too, belongs to the image of God as Ruler: "Great, Mighty, and Awesome."

The language of kingship as applied to God is not only that of fear and awe. A dimension of *trust* is a great part of this relationship as well. This aspect of the royal metaphor is not properly appreciated by the many in our day who reject this language. The King who made us knows what is good for us. In giving us Torah, law or teaching, God guides us in the way we are to live. There are, to be sure, various ways to understand the relationship between God and Torah. But the images in our tradition that depict God as both *judge* and *teacher* express the wisdom and caring of God as Divine Ruler. There is much authority in Judaism, but it is authority based upon care and trust. The *love* between

Ruler and subject is also very much a part of the Jewish religious imagination. Loyalty and familiarity characterize this relationship, sometimes more (especially in the rabbinic sources) than fear and awe. Israel is often described in midrash as "the beloved of the King" or as "children of the palace," having an easy and intimate relationship with the One, who, at the same time, is the mighty and awesome Ruler. The greatest danger to a person's soul, says one Hasidic master, occurs when one forgets that one is the child of the King.

YETSIRAH: GOD AS PARENT

Eventually the consciousness of 'asiyah transcends itself and gives way to the insights of the second stage, yetsirah. The God of yetsirah is the loving parent. Here, too, the relationship derives from Creation (remember that 'asiyah, yetsirah, and beri'ah are all terms for "making" or "creating"), but now it is no longer the authority of divine rule that expresses the relationship between creature and Creator. Here God is the parent who creates, who brings forth a being who is "soul of My soul." Two verses in the Torah describe God's creation of human beings. One says, "God created the human in His image...male and female God created them" (Gen. 1:29). The other says that "God blew the breath of life into [Adam's] nostrils" (Gen. 2:7). The sages add that one who blows breath into someone else brings that breath forth from within his/her own self. Both of these accounts show the deep affinity between God and humanity, very much like that of parents who see themselves reflected within their offspring.

The God of yetsirah knows and loves us fully, the way only a parent can love a child. This is a God who accepts us as we are, with all of our shortcomings. However, the God of yetsirah is also a parent who cares enough to make demands on us. God as parent has not given up on us and maintains faith always in our ability to grow and change. God knows that this growth, if it goes far enough, will eventually bring us back to our deepest selves and to relationship with the One who is our Source. A trusting parent knows that any road the child takes will lead back home.

The symbol of the *yetsirah* world is the angel; this realm of consciousness is sometimes referred to as "the world of angels." The angel is an eternal child. Beloved of God, completely obedient in spirit, the innocent angel is called a cherub (*keruv,* in Hebrew; *ke-ravya* in Aramaic), a word said to mean "like a child." The angel represents that aspect of the human self that seeks to stand in God's presence and serve with a totally undivided heart. The self of *yetsirah* longs to be like the prophet who, on seeing the angelic vision, says, "Here I am, send me" (Is. 6:8). I am Your beloved child.

These two aspects of religious life comprise *yir'ah* and *ahavah,* the fear and love of God. For most of the faithful in prior ages, they represented the totality of devotional life. Indeed the classic works of Jewish ethical literature speak of achieving the proper balance between these two, the relationship with God requiring both the "left" side of *yir'ah,* a proper sense of awe and distance, and a "right" side of *ahavah,* a love expressed in faithful devotion and commitment. The two classic metaphors of Jewish nonmystical theology are found in the phrase *Avinu Malkenu,* "Our Father, our King," so familiar from the liturgy of the High Holy Days.

In all ages, the mystics have sought to go beyond these two levels of understanding. We sense a need for a still greater intimacy than that afforded by the embrace of God as a loving parent. We seek out those stages of religious development where the borders between the divine and human worlds reveal themselves as porous and finally begin to disappear. Today this interest in the deeper levels of consciousness extends far beyond the small elite circle of "mystics." Some turn to Kabbalah from an already developed path of meditation or contemplative growth, often fostered by religions of the East. In the more abstract forms of both the Hindu and Buddhist religions, conventional forms of devotion to the deity are left behind by the renunciate. As these traditions are presented to Westerners, they allow for inward growth without the stages we have just described. Many seekers, not attracted to the language of theism, have been able to attain great insight through such an approach. In turning to Kabbalah, seeking out a Jewish or Western language for the spiritual life, they do not want to return to the plane of duality, demanding the worship of God as "other."

Some seekers turn to Kabbalah precisely because submission to authority cannot serve as their foundation for religious life. Traditional religion's authority has been challenged by insights from several fronts, including those of biblical criticism, comparative religion, and psychology. These challenges make it easier for that part of our psyche, which in any case resists submission, to stake its claim. The very real issues raised by feminism are also part of this challenge. The maleness of these two central metaphors of Jewish theology, it is claimed, is not incidental. They combine to form a figure of God as the dominating Other, precisely the all-too-human figure experienced by women in their oppression in a male-dominated society. This burden of inequality makes a turn to the mostly male God-image of exoteric Judaism difficult for women who bear a strong feminist consciousness. While the oppressive character of religion has been laid bare by the struggles of feminists in our day, it is by no means only women who have suffered from it. The questions of providence and authority have rocked Judaism to its foundations over the course of the past century; many Jewish men as well as women have turned away from a religious language that no longer seems to "speak to them" for these reasons.

But now some of these seekers, Jews and others who do not see themselves as traditional "believers," are turning to Kabbalah in search of some deeper keys with which to unlock a truth that they know lies within their hearts. They have a glimmer of understanding that tells them that Kabbalah is a Judaism that goes beyond these images. They seek in the mystical tradition a Judaism that is nondualistic and not based primarily on images of either maleness or authority. We need to open a path to such a joyous and life-embracing Judaism. For these reasons and others, the number of seekers who want to go beyond these first two stages is much higher than it was in prior ages.

BERI'AH: GOD AS LOVER

The third world, called beri'ah, is also one where love is the dominant motif in the relationship between God and person, but with an important difference. The parent-figure of yetsirah is now replaced by God the lover. This is a love between God and the soul in which eros is fully given its due. In Hebrew it would be called ḥeshek, or "passion." The key text for this beri'ah relationship is the Song of Songs, the Bible's passionate series of love poems, described by the great first/second-century teacher Rabbi Akiva as the "holy of holies" among the Scriptures. This lovers' canticle has always had a special place in mystical Judaism. Recited each Friday evening by Sephardic and Hasidic Jews, it was a text known by heart in prior generations. Commentaries to the Song of Songs are an important part of the kabbalistic legacy. The Zohar, the most passionate work of kabbalistic teaching, refers to verses from the Song of Songs with great frequency.

In the 'asiyah stage, we lived fully within our separate identities. In yetsirah, we considered our individuation as we saw ourselves both linked to, and separated from, God as parent, just as we struggle around issues of individuality and separation with our human parents. Now in beri'ah we give vent to our longing for reunion with the Source, the embrace of our soul in the arms of the Beloved. "I hold fast to him and will not let him go until I have brought him to the house of my mother, into the chamber of her who gave me birth" (Song of Songs 3:4). The desire to open to God as beloved does to lover, to be filled with God's presence as the lover is filled, is one that allows no holding back.

The *beri'ah* experience as we are describing it here is not one that we find readily discussed in most Jewish sources outside of Kabbalah. High value is given to modesty in Judaism's spiritual life, reflecting the restrained sexual mores of the tradition. Those who achieved or sought out the passionate intensity of life with God did not speak about it easily, and took great caution in prescribing it for others. Nevertheless, if one knows where to look in the sources, whether in the old books of mystically inspired "ethical teachings" or in the later writings of Hasidic masters, it can be found. "Great love until the soul passes out," it is called by the first rabbi of Lubavitch. It reverberates from the lines of *Yedid Nefesh*, "Soul's Beloved," a pietist love poem that is customarily chanted just before welcoming the Sabbath:

Soul's Beloved, compassionate Father,

Draw Your servant to Your will.

Let him run, swift as a deer,

To kneel before Your majesty.

Sweeter is Your love to him

Than honey from the comb,

Than any taste of pleasure.

Glorious, radiant, cosmic light,

My soul is faint for love of You.

Heal her, I pray, O God,

Show to her Your splendorous glow.

Then she will be strengthened, cured,

Your maidservant forever.

O Faithful, may Your tender mercies

Reach Your son who loves you greatly.

In deepest longing has he sought

To gaze upon Your mighty splendor.

My God, my heart's delight,

Come quickly: be not hidden.

Reveal Yourself, my dearest;

Spread over me the shelter of Your peace.

Your presence lighting up the world,

We shall rejoice, exult in You.

Hurry, Lover, time has come!

Grant me Your grace

As You did of old.[1]

The poem is not a kabbalistic one in the specific sense; it does not refer to *sefirot*. It speaks directly to God, whose name Y-H-W-H is to be found in the opening letters of the four Hebrew stanzas. As is frequently the case in documents that reflect a real living faith, here we see the stages flow in and out of one another. The author's God is at once parent, spouse, and lover, but the poem is a highly passionate one, reminiscent of parallels found in Sufi or Hindu Bakhti religious poetry. Also striking here is the personal, yet universal, quality of the appeal. Were this poem not written in Hebrew, we would not know for certain in which religious tradition it had been composed. Nor would it matter.

Kabbalah represents the full restoration of passion to the love life of God and the Jewish devotee. This is the great contribution of the *Zohar*, one of the most powerful works of mystical eros ever created. The *Zohar* is the masterwork of Kabbalah; all other kabbalistic books pale in comparison to its beautiful and mysterious teachings. The entire atmosphere of the work is fraught with erotically charged religious energy, and the love of male and female is the primary lens through which its "companions," as the mystics are called, view the experience of God's love as well.

One who seeks out this path of ḥeshek must understand that not all religious moments are the same. Shabbat and weekdays have their place in the healthy and well-balanced spiritual constitution. There are times of great intensity and there are moments when the ordinary and everyday is the proper lens through which to see God's presence in our lives. The masters of Jewish devotion like to paraphrase a line from the prophet Ezekiel's vision so that it says, "The life-force ebbs and flows" (Ezek. 1:14). There are moments when we are filled with spirit and seem to fly to great heights; there are others when we cannot imagine that such moments are real or even possible. In our own humility we begin to doubt the insights that came to us at the best of times. The only good advice for such a life is probably to acknowledge the spiritual roller coaster, to buckle our seat belts, hold on to someone we love, and enjoy the ride. Eventually we may come to learn that the ebb and flow are to be expected. Although (for better and worse) they are not regular or predictable, in the long run we accept them as inevitable. My own religious life has taught me to understand my inner self as being more like an ocean than like a calm lake. In accepting that, I let the ebb and flow of inspiration feel like the rise and fall of spiritual tides, something it would be foolish to try to fight.

ATSILUT: BEYOND THE BOUNDS OF SELF

The fourth "world" or stage in spiritual growth is called atsilut, emanation or flow of divine grace. Rather little can be said about this stage, as it is the most impenetrable to language. The original home of the sefirot and of the inward journey, it is that place beyond all places toward which our entire journey has been leading. It is the place beyond love, the innermost heart where the flames of passion are cooled. In atsilut there is no longer a need to speak of love between the self and God, because "between" no longer exists. "You" are not other than God. This is the place of "there is nothing else," referred to earlier; the flow of life has utterly overwhelmed the separate self. God knows us in *atsilut* as God's own self; the Knower, the knowledge, and the known are entirely one, indistinguishable from one another.

Within the divine universe, the "world" of *atsilut* exists forever, indeed in a realm beyond both time and space. Our journey to it perforce takes us across both of those boundaries and allows us to touch eternity and universality—the all-present as it *is*. Within the human mind, however, *atsilut* is usually present only in brief moments, in flashes of insight that pass quickly in themselves, but remain with us in memory to light the rest of our lives.

In our day, many people have had access to experiences that touch the world of *atsilut* through the use of LSD or other psychedelic drugs. Such experiences can indeed be valuable in opening the mind to the reality of higher consciousness. As one who tried psychedelics after some years of studying the kabbalistic and Hasidic masters, I found that the drug-induced experiences confirmed a great deal of what I had found in their writings. I also became wary of the dangers connected to this path, particularly as I saw it cheapened and degraded in popular culture. More people came to psychedelics after watching violent movies or listening to ear-blasting music than did after studying the mystical masters. Those people seemed to find in the experience confirmation of *their* own prior mindset. Some were led further down the path of violence and self-destruction. I continue to believe that such tools may be of great value, but only in carefully controlled settings in tandem with, and never instead of, the disciplines refined through many generations of mystical practice. (It should be noted that the use of LSD and other psychedelic drugs is still illegal.)

Atsilut is beyond striving, even beyond "experience," which itself implies a self that undergoes the experience. It happens to us in what can only be described as moments of grace, this-worldly foretastes of that paradise where the Oneness of God will be

whole, unchallenged by the stirring of any separate self, the time
of which the poet wrote:

ואחרי ככלות הכל לבדו ימלוך נורא

והוא היה והוא הוה והוא יהיה בתפארה

God in awe will reign again, when it all is done,

Was, Is, and Will Be. Endless glory. One.[2]

6

Shemot: The Way of Names

SPEAKING THE INEFFABLE

KABBALAH IS A PATH OF INSIGHT. Its greatest creation is its symbolic language, the essential structures of which we have just discussed. The *sefirot* and *'olamot* as outlined here have taken us only on the first step of a journey into the kabbalist's mind. Each of the ten *sefirot* is described by a host of symbolic terms, and it is the links created among these symbols that make Kabbalah such a profound and powerful tool for contemplative expansion of the mind. To follow the path of the kabbalists is to learn this language and to enter into the world of associative thinking that it inspires. The mystical experience that lies at the heart of Kabbalah is conveyed through these symbolic patterns.

The kabbalists understand that they are treading into the realm of the ineffable. The reality and truths to which they seek access lie beyond expression in language as we usually employ it. Absolute and irreducible reality, which is the mystic's goal, is not readily contained in words. They therefore set out to create a different way of speaking, a language that is able to reach and give expression to these higher levels of reality or deeper rungs of human consciousness. For this purpose, it is most useful to think of the *sefirot* not as some sort of cosmic "entities," but as *clusters of symbolic associations,* the mention of any of which (whether in daily life, in speech, or in a text) automatically brings to mind all the others as well. For this purpose, the conventional names of the *sefirot* (*keter, ḥokhmah, binah,* etc.) have no particular importance; they are simply one more layer within the complex network of associated symbols.

Let us take an example that will illustrate this concept. We have seen that the third *sefirah,* conventionally called *binah,* is described as a palace filled with light. This is the "upper palace," the first home of the divine light, parallel to *shekhinah,* the "lower" or final palace into which the light flows. As such, *binah* is also the higher Tabernacle or the "First Temple." This *sefirah* is also the womb out of which the seven sefirotic "days" are born. *Binah* is the one to whom all return, and she is thus called primal Mother (*imma 'ila'ah*). The fruitful mother of many is associated with Leah, the "higher" and more hidden spouse of Jacob. Because we long to go back to her, she is also *teshuvah* ("returning" to God). As the Mother of the seven lower *sefirot,* each of which is linked to all the others (7 x 7=49) she is identified with the jubilee (*yovel*), the fiftieth year when the Land, according to the Torah, returns to its original owner. So too do we long to return to our true "Owner," the Source from which we have come. The jubilee association with the fiftieth year also links *binah* with the holiday of Shavu'ot (Pentecost, the fiftieth day after Passover) and thus the revelation of Torah, which is the manifestation of the seed of *ḥokhmah* hidden within her. Still, the word *binah* does mean "understanding," and it is clear that we are speaking about a distinct aspect of mental activity as well, the contemplative understanding out of which the hidden Torah or the secret mind of God is revealed in us. Related to this is the image of *binah* as the quarry out of which the lower *sefirot* and the letters are hewn, just as speech is "engraved" in the mind. Similarly, she is the upper

Eden out of which the sefirotic rivers flow, the spring from which the waters of life are drawn.

We could continue to enrich this list by a host of other verbal pictures. These associations, when written out in the form of a list, will give us the following: Palace, First Temple, Upper Tabernacle, Mother, Womb, Leah, Understanding, Jubilee, Return, Source, Quarry, Eden, Spring, Shavu'ot, Fifty.

For the kabbalist, each time any of these words appears in the text—in the Torah or the prayerbook, for example—all the other terms are evoked and come to mind as well. The same thing happens whenever we see or experience any of the natural phenomena that are part of these clusters. To come upon a spring would thus be to think also of *teshuvah*, of the quarry, of the mysterious fifty, and of the Source of life. Encountering the word "quarry" in a text would immediately conjure mental pictures of the Mother, the jubilee, the spring, and all the rest. In this way, thinking, reading the sacred text, and the experience of daily life itself are all highly enriched by the patterns of association. This is kabbalistic thinking. To be a kabbalist is to live on the rarified mental plane engendered by such thinking.

What then *is* this third *sefirah*? True, the kabbalists think of it as a distinct stage in the divine journey from utter hidden Oneness toward divine self-revelation. It is also a specific level of mind or human contemplative experience. Likewise, *binah*, along with all the other *sefirot*, may also be viewed as a *cluster of symbols*, a nugget of enriched speech, by which the kabbalist can seek to express something of this deeper-than-accessible reality. The reality toward which *binah* points is the nexus of all of these symbols, hinted at in each of them and yet transcendent to them all.

It is no accident that each of these clusters of association contains within it symbols derived from the biblical text and Jewish tradition, personal figures, and representations of the world of nature. In striving for a language that would evoke a response from more profound levels of the human soul, the kabbalists rediscovered the great power of natural symbols. Including such terms as sun and sky *(tif'eret)*, moon, sea, and earth *(malkhut)*, dawn and dusk *(ḥesed and gevurah)* in their symbolic repertoire added greatly to the feeling of depth and grandeur evoked by each of the symbolic clusters. Rabbinic Judaism had mostly turned its eye away from the magnificent evocations of God's wonders in Creation so stirringly described by the Psalms and prophets. For the Rabbis, the greatness of God was primarily to be seen in the profundities of Torah and its interpretation rather than in the beauties of nature. Kabbalah seeks to recreate a "cosmic spirituality," one that sees the wondrous miracle of Creation as testament to God's glory. The mystics turn with great frequency and passion to texts from those parts of the Bible that celebrate God's handiwork in Creation. The writings of those ancients poets are fed directly into the network of terms and associations that comprise kabbalistic symbolism.

Both Torah and life experience are thus viewed through a new symbolic prism. The potential for holiness is spread widely through our lives, as almost anything we encounter may belong to one or another of these clusters of association and will take us back to contemplating God. This is especially true of language, the sacred vehicle of both divine and human speech. Kabbalah was conceived by people who possessed a great love of language, especially of Hebrew, the sacred tongue. Every word and letter of Torah, indeed every vowel point and cantillation sign, points to great mysteries and needs to be treated with reverence. References to the hidden but ever-discoverable inner life of God are strewn throughout the text of the Torah, just as they are waiting to be revealed in the text of our lives.

THE ACT OF NAMING

Most highly valued of all are the names of God scattered through the Torah. Like the midrashic masters who came before them, the kabbalists paid careful attention to the varied names for God and sought to link these to their own symbolic understanding. One of the richest veins to explore within Kabbalah is that of meditation on the names of God. This practice is rooted in some of the most ancient and universal teachings of religion, and versions of it are to be found in all the great traditions. It has a venerable place within Judaism, one that lay mostly dormant for centuries but is being avidly rediscovered in our own day.

To speak or contemplate the name of God is to stand in relation to God. It is to know the universal One in a *personal* way. "I know your name" means that I can speak to you; I possess the word that will cause you to look up and respond when I call out. This personal dimension of calling upon God's name is essential for the Jewish religious quest. Judaism insists that the secret of existence is a *"Who?"* not a *"What?"* question. Knowing God's name is therefore a matter of intimacy; to speak it is an act of love. We call it out the way a lover revels in the great delight of pronouncing a beloved's name. At the same time, the name of God represents a mystery, an inner essence of being that lies beyond our own powers of comprehension. Only insofar as God gives us the gift of opening our minds, do we begin to understand. Knowing and proclaiming God's name is a first key to unlock that understanding. The psalmist's God says, "I will raise him up because he knows my name" (Ps. 91:14). The uplifting comes from God.

Naming is also an act of great power. This aspect of stating a name reaches back to the very first stirrings of language, both in the collective history of humanity and in the life of the individual. The ability to name something is an act of mastery. By knowing what it is, we are able to control it. The child who learns to speak begins by naming things; in doing so he or she gains a measure of control not previously possessed. Both science and magic, each in its own way, may be seen as deriving from this insight. The scientist categorizes and classifies; this is a variety of control by naming. Knowing the species or genus to which a particular phenomenon belongs permits the prediction of behavior. This predictability, as one manipulates the circumstances, allows a measure of control. The magician exercises power in a less subtle way. Reciting the proper formula, a litany of names of angels or powers, is sufficient to transform reality, to rain down curses upon one's enemies, or to bless one's friends.

Kabbalah stands precisely at the powerful and dangerous meeting place between magic and religion. Implicit in its teachings is a notion of theurgy, or the belief that human words and deeds have the power to affect the cosmos and to bring divine blessing into the world. Because Kabbalah is firmly rooted in a great moral/religious tradition, this can never be an automatic power, as it is in magic. It is God's love, the divine desire to bless, that causes blessing to flow. The kabbalist is an agent who has been granted the privilege of having a small part in the cosmic process, the constant renewal of life and the endless flow of divine blessing or radiance into the world and into the human heart. This process goes through us and dwells within, but also reaches far beyond us. We are not its masters, but its servants. Our knowledge and insight are there to serve God's end, not our own.

We begin thinking about the names of God by considering the pronouns spoken by the divine voice, according to the biblical authors. The kabbalist understands Scripture as a living font of divine speech, a text through which God addresses each person. To enter into this mindset we need to go beyond our modern understanding of the texts' authorship and try to feel ourselves addressed by the voice that lies within them. The God who says "I" or "I am" represents *shekhinah*, or indwelling. This is the divine "I" that echoes through the universe, the palpable Presence of divinity. Wherever you stand, you stand within the "I am" of God.

God as *atah*, or "Thou," is the God of the intermediate *sefirot*, the forces that coalesce around *tif'eret* or the blessed Holy One. *Atah* represents the "male" energy within God, the one to whom *shekhinah* is partner. This is the God we meet as Other, the One before whom we stand in both love and judgment. *Atah* is the

God with whom we exist in relationship as with another. We address prayer to God as *atah,* even though we know that God's "I am" is also within us and all around us.

On the far side of this meeting of "I" and "Thou" is the God who can only be known by the hidden third person (in fact, the way you say "third person" in Hebrew grammar is *nistar,* "the hidden one"): God as He/She. This is the God of mystery: beyond calling, beyond direct address, beyond both love and awe, God as the hidden ground of all existence. All of these are aspects of the same God, experienced in different modes. The "I" of God, so apparent to one who lives in this world with eyes open, is our first source of inspiration, the One who sends us on our quest. We first discover God as indwelling Presence through the radiant beauty of the natural world or in the love of those to whom our hearts are open. This experience urges us to go onward, to seek out deeper levels of that same truth. In the course of seeking, we learn to become devotees, calling to God as "Thou," linking our needs and emotions to the search for God. Only in this way does the quest become one with life itself, a single journey of existence. Its goal, however, lies beyond the personal, leading us to stand face to face with the great Mystery, the Source to which we all return, the hidden One that has never been divided.

THE HOLIEST WORD

The proper name of God that we have been rendering in this book as Y-H-W-H is the most holy word in Judaism. It may not be spoken aloud, even in such sacred acts as prayer or the reading of the Torah. It may not be written down for any but the most holy purpose, and once written it may not be erased or discarded. Objects such as the Torah scroll, tefillin, or a mezuzah that have the holy Name written in them are the only objects that Jewish practice regards as truly holy. It has been customary since late biblical times to substitute the word *adonai,* or "my Lord," for the unspoken Name. "In this world," says God (in a well-known talmudic statement), "I am not called as I am written. I am written Y-H-W-H but called *adonai.* But in the world that is to come I will be both written and called Y-H-W-H."[1] The power to pronounce God's name fully and freely will come about only in the great future, when the world is redeemed. Or perhaps the power to know God so fully as to pronounce the Name will itself *be* the redemption for which we long. Meanwhile, living in this world, we may *think* the name Y-H-W-H, but we *say* it as *adonai.*

Adonai represents God as *shekhinah;* "She" turns to "Him" and says "my Lord." We, as her servants, do the same, but *adonai* is an outer form, a garment for the holy Name. Every time it is spoken, the name Y-H-W-H is contained within it. This symbolizes our situation as well: we turn to God in prayer as an "other," addressing the One in the words "blessed are *You.*" As we speak them, we know that God is fully present within us as well, that we too are naught but a garbing of the divine light.

Adonai is not an easy word for moderns to say. It is no wonder that some Jewish devotees in our time have taken to avoiding it, a practice I regret. It is true that to say "my Lord" seems like an act of fealty in a classic medieval master/servant sense, but to say it to God is a statement of submission, of accepting divine authority, and of coming to terms with the fact that we indeed have no ultimate mastery over our own fate. To say it breaks our proud modern heart, shatters our illusion that we are in control. That is why I believe it is still important for us to do so, perhaps more now than ever.

To say *adonai* while thinking Y-H-W-H makes each utterance of God's name a complex and energy-filled event. In the prayer-books of the kabbalists it is written as follows:

יְהֹוָ֫אֲדֹנָ֫י יֱאֲהֹדֹוִנָֽהִי

Here the letters Y-H-W-H and ADNY are joined together in two ways: first the letters ADNY are included in an expanded final "H" of Y-H-W-H, indicating that all the upper *sefirot* are to be found with *shekhinah*, who represents the final letter of God's name. Then the letters Y-H-W-H and ADNY are intertwined into the form of YAHDWNHY, representing the full union of male and female, *tif'eret* and *shekhinah*. Our access to the Divine always begins through *shekhinah*. Within that indwelling Divine Presence we discover all the higher rungs. As we open ourselves to them, *shekhinah* is raised through us, bringing about the union of "within" and "beyond."

The Name יְהֹוָה, Y-H-W-H, embraces the entire sefirotic world. The letter *yod*, smallest of the letters, represents *ḥokhmah* as primordial point, the beginning of existence. The tip of the *yod* points upward, hinting at *keter*, an essence so elusive that it cannot be captured in writing. The first *he*, graphically depicted as an open structure, is *binah*, primal female into which the *yod* enters. *Waw* stands for the number six, representing the six forces centered in *tif'eret*. It also represents an elongation of the *yod* and thus becomes a phallus-like embodiment of male energy within God. The second *he*, again female, is the home of the *waw*, the ark of the covenant, and also the home of the soul.[2]

A MEDITATION ON GOD'S NAME

It is time now for us to try out the simplest of all meditations on the name of God. It has probably occurred to you that the letters Y-H-W-H are all "soft" sounds, midway between consonants and vowels. In fact, they constitute nothing harder than the breath itself. This mysterious name of God may not be spoken, but it may be breathed.

> *Prepare yourself for meditation. Sit with eyes closed, breathing quietly. When you are ready, begin to breathe through your open mouth. Without sound, shape your lips just slightly to form a "y"-like breath on the intake. As you breathe out, the voiceless "h"-sound will be quite natural. On the next breath,*

*form your lips in just a slightly different way to breathe in a "w."
Then breathe out again, "h." Do not recite the names of the
letters ("yod, he"), but just silently breathe in and out the sound
of each letter. Thus you are breathing the name of God.*

*Nothing could be simpler. God is as natural as the breath of
life. You are breathing the name of God. Continue, breathing
in and out through the mouth, gently forming the "y" and "w"
on the intake breaths. As you enter into the process, you may
carry the images of the sefirot with you in your breathing. On
"y," reach inward toward hokhmah, source of all, transcendent
mystery. On "h," hokhmah breathes out to binah, birthing all
the energies. Your "w" reconcentrates these as the six directions, or "days," of activity all come together as the "male" principle, entering again into "h" as shekhinah, God throughout the
world and within your soul.*

*Breathe in, breathe out. Y-H-W-H. When you are ready, let go
of the concentrated oral breaths. Breathe naturally, but continue to be aware. This is the moment to acknowledge that all
breath is the breathing in and out of God's name, that to live,
by the simple fact of breathing, is to recite the name of God.
This is the conclusion of the psalmist: "Every breath praises
God. Halleluyah!"*

Remember that we are not permitted to pronounce God's
name aloud. The Name is too holy for our so readily profaned lips,
but it may—indeed it should—dwell within our hearts. Have a
shiviti, or meditation chart, in the place where you pray, to help
you focus on the Name. Keep it within you as the unspoken word.
Have it stand as a constant challenge to everything else you say.

There are countless more complex ways to meditate on the
divine Name, some of which you will undoubtedly discover as you
learn more of Kabbalah. Many authors comment on the
numerical value of the name (twenty-six) and attribute secret
meanings to it. Both the words *ahavah* ("love") and *ehad* ("one")

are numerically thirteen; love and oneness joined thus make up the name of God. Kabbalists also take a great interest in differing expansions of the name Y-H-W-H, derived by filling out its letters (reading them as *yod, he, waw, he*), spelled in various ways. Thus they derive 45, 52, 63, and 72 as each equaling one version of God's name. Others supply the Name with different vowel points, each reading directed toward a distinct focus of meditation. The kabbalists of the old Jerusalem school called Bet El have a prayerbook that is composed almost entirely of permutations of the four letters of God's name, through which the entire worship service is transformed into a highly complex symphony of meditations. There is hardly a person outside their small circle who is capable of reading and understanding that text. My own taste within contemplative practice is for steadiness and simplicity. I urge you to go slowly in adopting more elaborate meditative exercises. Find a simple path, this one or another, and be faithful to it. A word to the wise is sufficient.

ELOHIM: THE MANY WITHIN THE ONE

Another Hebrew term for God, often used as a Divine Name, is *elohim*. This is the generic Hebrew word for "god," and it is used in the Torah to describe both the One in whom we place our faith and the "false" gods of those "heathens" who were Israel's enemies in ancient times. *Elohim* is also occasionally used in the sense of "great one," referring to a respected human authority.

The most interesting thing about *elohim* is the fact that it is a plural form. A singular *(eloha)* does exist, but Scripture almost never uses it. The Bible acknowledges the plural form of *elohim* when using it to speak of "other gods," and plural verbs or adjectives are used with it, as required by the rules of proper grammar. When the same plural word is used to refer to the God of Israel, those rules are intentionally violated and *elohim* is treated as though it were singular. Thus the Bible's opening words *bereshit bara' elohim* ("In the beginning God created...") are something of a grammatical abomination! Every time the Torah says *va-yomer elohim* ("God said"), the rules of grammar are broken.

This is, of course, no accident. The point is that *elohim* in this context is being used as a *collective*. All of the powers that once belonged to the deities of the pantheon—love, power, wisdom, war, fruitfulness, and all the rest—are now concentrated in this single Being who contains them all. The blessings needed for every aspect of human life all come from a single source. Your nation's God and mine are also one in this all-embracing deity. This is the essence of the monotheistic revolution, embodied in the language each time you use this common Hebrew word for "God."

The kabbalists offer another secret connected to the word *elohim*. They read the word as composed of two shorter Hebrew terms: אלה/*eleh* and מי/*mi*, meaning "these" and "who." "These" refers to the seven lower *sefirot* or "aspects" of the divine Self. By extension, it includes all our images, ideas, and descriptions of God. "These" are as varied as are the sacred languages of humanity; every one of them contains some aspect of truth, but all are incomplete. "Who" stands for *binah*, the secret that defies all description, the God of transcendent mystery. No words or images can describe this God, the One who is only question, not answer. The first great homily of the *Zohar* quotes the prophet Isaiah: "Raise your eyes to heaven and see *who* created *these*" (Is. 40:26). Mystery and images are one. *Mi* and *eleh* have to be joined. Only together do they comprise אלהים/*elohim*. And here the *Zohar* warns us severely of the dangers of idolatry. Those who worshipped the Golden Calf, it reminds us, called out: "*These* are your gods, O Israel!" (Ex. 32:4).

Following the ancient teachings of the Rabbis, the mystics often assign the name *elohim* to the side of judgment, while Y-H-W-H refers to the God of love. The occurrence of the two names together, as they are often found in the Bible, provides an opportunity for the drawing of judgment toward *ḥesed*, one of the kabbalists' most important mystical intentions. Yes, we all know and recognize the need for balanced judgment. Still, our task is always on the humanizing side, that of pulling justice under the sway of compassion. "Including the left within the right," or subsuming judgment under the power of love, is one of the chief *kavvanot* (mystical "intentions") of kabbalistic teaching.

Balanced judgment is one of the most important meanings assigned to the *Shema'*, the proclamation of God's unity that pious Jews recite twice each day. There, the word *elohenu*, "our God," is found between two occurrences of Y-H-W-H. So are we to overwhelm the forces of judgment with those of love and compassion, surrounding them on all sides, until they are "sweetened" and transformed. Thus will *elohim*, the divine force of justice, become *elohenu, our* God, the *shekhinah* present within our hearts.

ONE GOD, MANY NAMES

The Hebrew language, both biblical and later, is as rich with names of God as the Eskimo tongue is supposedly blessed with terms for snow. Each Name found in the Torah is linked with one or another of the *sefirot*, in ways that vary from one kabbalistic school or author to another. The name *El*, for example (well known to us from the endings of such angel-names as Micha-*el*, Rapha-*el*, etc.), is most often ascribed to *hesed*, demonstrating the love of God. So too is it linked to *hod*, our grateful acknowledgment of reality. When joined to *'elyon*, or "exalted," to form *El 'Elyon*, a name we use in our *'amidah* prayer (see below), it can refer either to *keter* or *binah*, a force more exalted and hidden than the seven "lower" aspects of divinity. *El* combined with *Shaddai* (often translated "Almighty," but read in Kabbalah as "fulfilled") either indicates the joining of *yesod* and *malkhut*, the flow of divine energies into the Mother of the lower world, or hints at the unity of *keter* and *malkhut*, the complete Oneness of the revealed and hidden God.

I hesitate for two reasons to offer a more detailed account of the names of God in Kabbalah. First, I fear overloading you with information. Remember that this book's purpose is not a conveying of information in detail, but the setting out of a spiritual path. Kabbalah was destroyed in the past by excessive preoccupation with the details of an over-elaborated system. This was especially manifest in an extremely complex system of meditations on the Name, in nearly infinite permutations, vocalizations, and so forth. Let us be aware of the trap of "information overload" and avoid falling into it. Second, the use of names beyond those discussed above has not been an important part of my own path, which this book is meant to share and convey. I have found much fulfillment in meditating on the great name Y-H-W-H in very simple ways, and have not wanted—or needed—to go down the much more complicated paths offered by many kabbalistic teachers. I do not find those ways wrong or faulty; they simply are not suited to my own spiritual temperament or need. To offer them to you here would lead me away from faithfulness to my own experience, which is the cornerstone of all that I have to teach.

PART II

Looking Toward Tomorrow

7

Seeking a Path

TURNING INWARD

T HIS BOOK IS ALL ABOUT the inner journey, yours and mine.
Kabbalah should be seen as an ancient Jewish roadmap for
undertaking this journey. Like any map, it cannot get you there
on its own. Guided by the map, *you* still have to do the walking.
You have to put in the effort, overcome the fatigue and disap-
pointments that come along the way. You have to deal with those
obstacles that no map could possibly point out, as they belong to
you alone.

Why is it important here to emphasize the inner journey?
Because Kabbalah, as we have often described it, still seems to be
a map of the cosmos, and only secondarily a diagram of the
human mind. In speaking of "worlds," of the contraction of
the divine Self, of primal space, and all the rest, the texts speak
the language of cosmology, of world-ordering, rather than of in-
wardness, of soul-ordering.

The Hasidic masters understood that the true value of kabbalistic teaching was in the spiritual-psychological realm. While
they by no means denied or even questioned the truth claims of

Kabbalah as a metaphysic, their interest was always in the ways in which kabbalistic concepts could be used to explain the human mind, both spiritually and emotionally. In reading the Torah as well as the works of previous mystical masters, they sought to approach everything *al derech ha-'avodah,* "in the way of service." Theirs is a practical rather than a theoretical mysticism. "How can this concept, verse, or teaching help me to understand myself, so that I can better serve God?" was their constant question. We follow in their footsteps, but in a framework appropriate to our age.

Because we come to the mystical tradition bearing a legacy of modernity, our questions and assumptions are necessarily different than those of either the original kabbalists or the Hasidic masters. We no longer claim to understand the nature of the universe through any grand metaphysical system. It is to the physicist rather than the philosopher that we turn for questions about cosmic origins. Modern philosophy, ever since Immanuel Kant, has questioned our ability to make objective claims about the nature of reality that are not limited by the conceptual categories created by our limited human mind. As post-moderns coming back to a spiritual tradition created in pre-modern times, our claims to truth must be more modest than those of our ancestors. We can understand and appreciate roadmaps for the mind. We can test such maps by using them in our own journeys and see how well they work for us. We can even make some adjustments in those ancient maps—the largest of these in our age will surely be the new women's contributions and reroutings—to make them work better for us. As to whether these maps are also mirrors of a cosmic reality—that is to say "Truth" with a capital "T"—such a claim may remain beyond us. We can only report on our own experience and the profound effect these teachings have had upon us.

To say that the kabbalists' insights are useful chiefly for mapping the inner landscape is not, however, to reduce all of Kabbalah to psychology. Our discussion of the *sefirot* has suggested a subtle interplay between the faith that we are created in God's image and the degree to which we see images of God as projections of our own human reality. The purpose of using kabbalistic insights on the psychological plane is to point toward a *transcendental psychology,* an understanding of human personality as emerging out of a deep well of pre-conscious reality. That well draws on sources that are truly infinite, rooted in a mysterious inner self that ties us to all others and to the single Self of the universe.

WHAT IS THE SOUL?

The word *soul* appears several times in this book. I hesitate to define the term, because almost any definition renders it sounding like an "entity" or "thing" hidden somewhere within the brain. And that is precisely what "soul" is not. Just as Y-H-W-H is not a "thing," but refers rather to the transcendent totality of being that both embraces and surpasses all things, so is the soul like a transcendent wholeness of the person, a mysterious essence that is more than the sum of all the characteristics we could name about that person.[1]

The main Hebrew term for "soul" is *neshamah,* actually meaning "breath." When the Torah depicts God blowing the breath of life into Adam's nostrils (Gen. 2:7), Adam becomes a "living being," a bearer of soul. Our soul comes into being in the moment when God breathes life into us. That moment, we come to understand, is *every* moment. God is constantly blowing the breath of life into us. We are being created anew, reborn, in each moment.

Neshamah is that breath. It is the place of connection between God and person, or between the small self of individual identity and the great Self of being. It is the aspect of us that never separated from our Source, that did not let go of its divine root in the course of that long process of individuation and alienation that we call human life. As difficult as it is to find that place of inner connection to the cosmos and all that is, I believe that it is present within each of us. The "journey" to God is thus nothing other than a return to our deepest self. The task is to seek out that innermost reality, to find it, and to reshape the rest of our lives around that return.

KAVVANAH: THE PURPOSE OF OUR QUEST

What is the purpose of it all? Why are we seeking to recover Kabbalah? Ours is a quest for da'at, best translated in this context as "awareness." We understand the entire religious life as intended to cultivate an awareness that the world is filled with divine radiance, that each moment can be a Sinai for the one whose heart and mind are open. This is an inward-looking transformative vision, one that goes out to the world through a path that first turns inward to create a different quality of perception and receptivity. Awareness here means insight, an inward view of all things, that gives us the ability to see all outer forms as levushim, or garments that clothe the divine light. Each of these forms does so in its unique way, but the radiance that inhabits and enlivens them is all one.

We uncover the Presence within all things and within ourselves. Seeing yourself as an embodiment of divine light enables you to see the world that way, and vice versa, but insight, as important a goal as it is, must also come to be understood as a means rather than an end. Our return to the One is not a matter of self-discovery alone. It demands the reshaping of our lives in response to that inward learning. This reshaping has implications for as many dimensions as there are in our lives: our marriages or primary relationships, the way we relate to our children, our parents, our friends. It should affect decisions about career, about the pace of our lives, about where we live and how we live. Da'at (insight) brings us to teshuvah (return); teshuvah leads us to ru'ah ha-kodesh (cultivation of the holy spirit).

I believe with true Hasidic faith that every person is capable of this understanding and the redemption that comes from it, each in his/her own way. Our task in life is to spread such awareness as widely and as deeply as we can throughout humanity. The closest Hasidism has to a founding document or statement of purpose is a letter written by the Ba'al Shem Tov (1700–1760), the movement's first central figure, to his brother-in-law, who was living in the Holy Land.[2] He tells there of an experience of "soul-ascent," in which he was taken up into the heavens and shown great visions, most of which he was forbidden to recount. In the course of his journey, he encountered the messiah, and he asked him the eternal question: "When will you come?" The answer: "When everybody can attain the Oneness of God as you have, when your experience is shared throughout humanity—that will be the time of the redemption." We still have a little bit of work to do.

In the words of another Hasidic master, the Rabbi of Chernobyl:

> It is the Creator's will, blessed be His name, that every person attain to the primal word, that of which it says "By the Word of God the heavens were formed." The entire Torah is included in that single word, one that no mouth can speak.[3]

This is a deeply universal teaching. It understands that there is a primal revelation, that of the single word, prior to all specific revelations, including our own Torah. All revelations are living truth only insofar as they serve as arks to contain and preserve that single word, their true source of energy and inspiration. In that sense both exclusivity ("Ours is the only *true* religion") and triumphalism ("Ours is the *best* religion") are distortions of reality and obstacles to the work we must do. The *One* as primal word needs to be accessible to all people in a cultural form that they can call their own; indeed the single Word of God must be implanted and discoverable in every human spiritual "language." To think any less would be to diminish or limit the holy spirit.

MYSTICISM FOR TODAY'S SEEKER

Here we should say a bit more about the term *mysticism*, asking ourselves what we mean when we think of ourselves as followers of a "mystical" path within Judaism. The word *mysticism* itself is of Greek and Christian origins and is therefore not native to the traditions of which we speak, none of which saw themselves as "mystical." The equivalent Hebrew terms—*sod* ("secret"), *ḥokhmah nistarah* ("hidden wisdom"), *kabbalah* ("tradition")— refer to the esoteric nature of these teachings, rather than their contents. Mysticism is generally taken to describe a certain category of religious *experiences,* and secondarily all the theology, textual sources, religious movements, and so forth that derive from them. Applying the term "mysticism" to the Jewish sources thus requires some adjustment in its usage and certain reservations about the meanings implied.

Mystics share with other religious people an intense awareness of Divine Presence and a constant readiness to respond to that presence in both prayer and action. For the mystic, that presence is revealed through powerful and transformative inner experiences. These seem to come from a source that lies beyond the ordinary human mind; they are usually understood as a divine gift, as a source of special favor or grace, as an act of revelation. The intensity of these experiences lends a sense that the consciousness they represent is a deeper source of ultimate truth than ordinary or "external" human experience.

Much has been written in recent years, both by scholars and practitioners, about the nature of mysticism. Various characteristic types of mystical experience have been outlined and shown to exist across the borders that historically define religious traditions and separate them from one another. Some of these experiences represent a slowing down of mental activity to a more restful and contemplative pace; others result from a speeding up of the mind in a rush of ecstatic frenzy. Some mystics describe a fullness of Divine Presence that overwhelms and floods the mind, while others speak of utter emptiness, a mind that becomes so devoid of content that it can transcend its own existence. Some mystics see their experiences conveyed by beings outside themselves: God, angels, or heavenly voices speak to them. Others may view the experience more internally: a deeper level of the soul is activated, revealing truths or insights that the person was unable to perceive when in an ordinary state of mind.

Most of these experiences, as described by those who undergo them, contain some element of striving toward oneness, a breaking down of illusory barriers to reveal the great secret of the unity of all being. Here we would do well to recall the parable of the Ba'al Shem Tov quoted earlier (see p. 19). This image could serve as a good opening for a discussion of mysticism in a Jewish context. The mystic is the one who sees through all the outer veils, who is not turned aside from the quest even by the beauties of religious experience itself. The true seeker is the one who knows that "there is nothing there but the King." The nature of this Oneness and its relationship to the phenomenal world that appears before us is described in a great variety of ways, depending both upon the personality of the individual mystic and the theology of the tradition out of which he or she speaks.

Many types of mystical experience and techniques of attaining it are represented within the rich legacy of Jewish mystical sources. The history of Jewish mysticism reveals a variety of experiences as well as widely differing styles of recording and discussing them. Kabbalah, as I wish to present it here, is a mysticism of the contemplative sort. The essential act of such a path is one of deep reflection upon the essential truths: the nature of being, the self, the purpose of our existence, the world around us. The contemplative life calls upon us to take the time required for a slow and richly textured examination of these matters. Torah and tradition provide the language and stimulus for that contemplation. We contemplate these not as an end in themselves, but as a way of opening the mind to go beyond the places where it usually dwells. As we persist in training the mind in this direction, we are privileged to have "new" levels of consciousness open up before us, rungs of perception that we had not previously known.

By traveling along these pathways of the contemplative mind, we come to catch a glimpse, perhaps just for a moment, of the underlying truth that all exists within the Oneness that is God. Kabbalah is both a pathway toward attaining this truth and a language for articulating it.

RELIGIOUS PRACTICE: KABBALAH AND COMMANDMENT

Now that we have learned something of kabbalistic language and gained a glimpse of the inner universe of the Jewish mystics, we turn back to the question of our own religious lives. Living in such a different world than that of the original kabbalists, we must ask ourselves how their teachings will translate into a Judaism suitable for our day.

This question takes us directly to the topic of spiritual practice. Is there something in particular one has to *do* in order to follow the wisdom of the kabbalistic masters? How do we *live* a mystical Judaism? This question is especially appropriate here because Judaism has always defined itself as a religion of deeds. The heart may indeed have great intentions and strive to reach the depths, but the value of its achievements will finally be measured in actions, in the way one's life is lived in the human and earthly community of which we are all a part.

Kabbalah has its origins within the heart of Judaism. The practice of Kabbalah is impossible to separate from classical Jewish practice, in which it is deeply rooted. Kabbalah did not develop a full-scale ritual or praxis of its own because Judaism was already so richly blessed with a life of religious deeds. Rather than separating themselves from the larger community and its religious life, kabbalists reinterpreted all of existing Jewish practice to deepen its meaning. The 613 commandments of the Torah (248 "do's" and 365 "don'ts") are viewed by the kabbalist as reflecting a secret inner structure, to be found in the cosmos as well as in the person, body and soul alike. The human being and the Torah, God's teaching, reflect the same truth and are thus parallel in structure to one another. To fulfill the commandments is to nourish one's soul; to transgress them is to do harm to one's own truest self. Even more, the performance of a *mitzvah*, a commanded duty, adds to the positive energy quotient in the universe. It is a gift we mortals can give to God, one that we trust is received in love. While Kabbalah itself means "receiving," it also trains us to be givers, to place our own acts of goodness on the altar that is always before us as we seek to stand in God's presence.

Every *mitzvah*, according to the kabbalists, has infinite meaning and limitless divine power. The commandments contain within them a secret life that gives expression to the mysterious inner structure of the universe. If we understand our own religious deeds properly, they serve as ways of pointing to the *sefirot*, or aspects of the divine Self, of which we shall soon have more to say. Mystical thought especially likes to wrap itself around certain of the more mysterious-seeming rituals of Jewish life. The blowing of the *shofar* on Rosh Hashanah, the waving of the *lulav* and *etrog* on Sukkot, the donning of tefillin for weekday prayers—these and other acts are seen as filled with sublime mysteries, and their performance gives strength to God, arousing the flow of divine energies that in turn allows blessing to flow into the world.

Kabbalah originally lived fully within the confines of traditional Judaism. The mystics added to the tradition, both in the special practices mentioned above and in their deeper understanding of the commandments. Sometimes there were slight variations between the mystics' practice and that of others, and these were occasionally even a source of tension. The kabbalists' devotion to the inner meaning of spiritual practice, however, was generally accompanied by very great care for every detail of halakhic ("legal," or proper) observance. That is still the way of the traditional Jerusalem-centered kabbalists of today.[4]

In our time, many seek to follow Jewish mystical teaching without assuming the full "yoke" of Jewish religious practice. Others may be open to trying, but cannot and often should not seek to absorb the tradition all at once. Step-by-step growth in practice is for most people a healthier and, in the long run, more stable way of approaching Halakhah, or the path of Jewish living. For some temperaments, especially those who struggle against being caught up in compulsive behavior, traditional religious practice can be especially difficult. The attention Judaism gives to the details of proper performance can be overwhelming and frightening, particularly for those who approach it from without, rather than having lived since childhood with regular and comfortable norms of Jewish practice.

It is important to remember that nobody, not even the seemingly most pious person, fulfills all the 613 commandments. First of all, it is logically impossible to do so. Many commandments applied only when the Temple in Jerusalem was standing, others relate only to one living in the Land of Israel. Some *mitzvot* may only be fulfilled by the high priest, an office that has been vacant for nearly 2,000 years. There are some commandments (although fewer these days!) that apply only to men, and others only to women. Therefore the sages said long ago that fulfilling the commandments is a collective obligation of the Jewish people.[5] We share the duties of tradition with one another as we share the joy in its rewards. We share the commandments with generations past and those yet to come. Each of us has to do our part as together, a community that transcends both time and space, we fulfill the Torah.

FINDING YOUR OWN *MITZVAH*

What is most important here is to maintain perspective. The *mitzvot* ("commandments") are instruments. Their purpose is to bring us to spiritual awareness and to serve as vehicles for our devotional life, vessels into which the abundance of spirit may be poured and momentarily contained. Hasidic teaching has always understood this: it sees the *mitzvot* as the living word of God, not merely the dictate of the *Shulḥan 'Arukh*, or Code of Jewish Law. Today's seeker may see the *mitzvot* and forms of Jewish worship as the gift of God or the legacy of tradition; neither origins nor authority is the central question for a living mystical faith. The important thing is that the forms stimulate us to open ourselves to that deeper place where we come to know, to love, and to serve the One within and all around us. Some of us will do so in an abundance of religious practices, unfolded in great detail. Others will be satisfied by more simple forms of religious life. These differences are affected by temperament, by training, and by past associations. They should never become a basis for judging one another, as none of us knows another's soul and the path it needs to take to come close to God. The important thing to remember is that, in acts of faith, quality rather than quantity counts. "One does more, another does less," teach the ancient sages, "the main thing is to direct your heart to heaven."[6] It may be that through a single deed you can add more to the treasures of divine light than is offered by endless hours of unfeeling practice by others.

An ancient tradition teaches that each Jew has a special *mitzvah* to perform, one that belongs to the unique root of that person's soul, and it is waiting for him or her to discover it. Even while fulfilling many of the commandments, you might want to devote some meditation to seeking out that special *mitzvah*, the place where you will shine a great light that is unique to who you are. It may be in some inter-personally based form of service that you will find a special devotion: helping the poor, welcoming guests, visiting the sick, or ministering to the dying. You may be more activist in your choice of *mitzvah*, working to bring peace, restore justice, or resolve conflicts between people. All of these are *mitzvot*, ways of embodying God's service, and we should see them as expressions of our devotion to the One, not "merely" as ways of helping others. Or you may find a ritual form that "speaks" to you more than any other. This may be something as frequent as rising at dawn for daily prayer or as infrequent and special as blowing the *shofar* on Rosh Hashanah or baking your own matzah on the eve of Passover. If your heart is open and your patience is great, you and your *mitzvah* will discover one another.

Still, you want (and need!) a path. Where to begin? What is it that I should do to practice a mystical Judaism for today? We will need to create in our time some simple norms of religious practice for Jews who seek a serious spiritual discipline short of the entirety of Jewish tradition. To do so is beyond the scope of this book, but a few somewhat personal suggestions are in order. There is an old Jewish custom of writing *hanhagot,* personal practices recommended by a teacher to a circle of disciples. A number of years ago, while studying some such texts, I wrote out my own series of personal instructions. I share them with you here.

These fourteen teachings are my own personal distillation of what I feel to be most essential for living a Jewish spiritual life in our day. You will note that they deal partly with *kavvanah,* matters of the heart, and partly with daily practices. They are by no means the be-all and end-all of Judaism, much remains to be explored and tried. In offering them to you I share a piece of my own path, partly as guidance for you, but in the greater hope that you will find *your* path, which will be somewhat different. I offer them as Halakhah, in the sense of a path on which to walk, rather than as absolute norms from which we never swerve. If you are looking for a place from which to begin, this is what I have to offer you.

A SIMPLE SERIOUS JUDAISM FOR TODAY

"These Are the Things a Person Should Do to Live by Them"

1. Know that all of life is holy, all exists within the One. There is no time or place in which God's presence cannot

be found. Meditate on this each day. Think about it at home, while commuting, at work, and back at home.

2. Take responsibility for your own spiritual life. It is we who lock God out of our lives. Therefore open your heart, train your heart to fill up with God's presence and God's love. Be aware in each moment, no matter where you are or what you are doing, of the divine radiance within you and all about you.

3. Train yourself to see the miracle of each day's arrival and departure. Celebrate the two sacred times of day, dawn and dusk, with prayer.

4. If your life is too complicated or too fast-paced to remain aware, work to live more simply and more slowly. Keep Shabbat as a time to slow down, live in harmony with nature, and reflect. Make room for that Shabbat consciousness to enter your weekday world as well. Slow down.

5. Live the rhythm of the sacred calendar—Shabbat, holidays, seasons—as rich with traditional forms or as simply as your spirit desires. Remember that it is you who has to fill those forms with God's presence. It is the joy of your spirit that brings them to life!

6. Study Torah every day. Choose those texts, methods of learning, classes, and study partners that make for a challenging and exciting learning experience. If learning Torah is dull, you are doing something wrong. If it is exciting to you, teach others.

7. Share with others the fullness of spirit that flows from your religious life. Give to others beyond measure, just as no one has measured the great gifts you receive. Give of yourself: give time, not just money; give directly, not just impersonally. Above all, give love.

8. Live in community with those who most closely share your path, but live in genuine openness to learning from others who do not. In choosing your life partner and friends, try to find those who will be open to and encourage your quest. Make space for spiritual awareness in your marriage or partnership. Talk about the holiness of your love, seeing it as a part of your love of God.

9. Recognize every person as the image of God. Work to see the Divine Image especially in those who themselves seem oblivious to it. Seek out the divinity in those who annoy, anger, or frustrate you. Hope to find and uplift sparks of holy light, even where it seems hardest. Do all the work that is needed to help others to discover the image of God within themselves.

10. Learn to recognize evil, usually a creation of frightened, selfish, or otherwise distorted human hearts. Always try to transform it, but be ready to confront it and to battle it with courage when there is no other choice.

11. Love the Jewish people, the root from which you are drawn. Work to improve the quality of Jewish life, both in Israel, where Judaism is most fully lived and tested in our day, and wherever you are. Contribute to the growth of Jewish life spiritually, intellectually, culturally, emotionally, in whatever way you can. Be part of the great healing process within the Jewish people, the repair of feelings and attitudes created by centuries of persecution and by the terrible holocaust of the past century, a healing that is not yet completed.

12. Work toward the expansion of the sacred into new realms, the creation of new religious forms appropriate to our age. Treat Judaism as a growing, dynamic tradition, one

that wants to creatively engage the future as much as it wants to preserve the legacy of the past.

13. Share the witness of God's Oneness with all who want to receive it. Witness by public prayer, by teaching, but mostly by doing. Be willing to share in mutual witness with those of other faith paths. Open your heart to be inspired by them, without losing confidence in the path that is your own.

14. Recognize once again that all of existence is divine. Devote yourself to the healthy preservation of life: your own, that of people around you, but also of all creatures on our much-threatened planet. Engage in the great collective *mitzvah* of our time, that of protecting this earth and its resources for generations that will come after us. Come to see humanity as part of the greater chorus of all creatures, each one an embodiment of divinity and a vital singer in life's great, complex, painful, but ultimately joyous and triumphant song: Halleluyah!

8

Great Chain of Being: Kabbalah for an Environmental Age

THE PRESENT HOUR

THE PRECEDING CHAPTERS of this book have gone from past to future. We have taken two key concept-structures of the old Kabbalah, *sefirot* and *'olamot,* and have offered contemporary interpretations of them, showing how they can be understood in a Kabbalah for tomorrow. We have shown how ancient names for God render their meaning in ways that may still speak to us in the very different world in which we live. Now it is time for us to work differently. Here we will begin not with the past but with the present, or even with a future that is already upon us.

We live in the shadow of environmental catastrophe. Two centuries of modernity have brought us tremendous scientific, technological, and medical progress. With this progress has come growth in human population, lengthening of the lifespan, and an unprecedented rise in comfort, convenience, and the standard of living. None of these blessings of modern life is to be regretted; we do not wish for a moment that humanity would again have to live without them. Indeed, we are deeply distressed at how unequally they are shared across the human race. Progress, however, has also exacted its price. The demands we have made on the world's natural resources, from the stripping bare of once-vast forests to the rapid emptying of fossil fuel reserves, stagger the mind. At the same time, the pollution of earth with the by-products of our endless desire for consumption—from carbon dioxide in the air, to the dangers of nuclear and chemical wastes, to the plain old choking of landfills with endless masses of plastic containers—threatens the existence of the simple, clean resources that future generations will need for survival: fertile soil, fresh air, drinkable water.

We are seeking to create a Kabbalah for a very particular age in the history of humanity. Our Kabbalah is a specifically Jewish teaching, to be sure, but it is no longer addressed to Jews alone, and it no longer sees only the history of the Jews as the context in which it lives. Our suffering planet is deeply and urgently in need of healing. We humans stand in a moment when we must find teachings that will change our way of life, if we and our world are to go on living. A Kabbalah for tomorrow has to be seen as a Jewish contribution to a universal quest, a part of the reclaiming of the great spiritual traditions of humanity, a resource much neglected in the West for the past several hundred years. These centuries of tremendous scientific progress and technological advance brought about a certain hubris in the Western mentality. Soon, we thought, science would teach us to conquer all! Both the physical limitations and the social ills of humanity would be wiped away by the ongoing progress of rational and scientific understanding.

It has taken the calamitous twentieth century to cure us of these illusions. The same science that conquered terrible diseases and took humans to the moon also brought us nuclear weapons and Zyklon B, the death-gas of Auschwitz. Progress itself has increased those demands that cause damage to our planet and lead to the depletion of its resources. We will need the collective wisdom of *all* of our traditions to guide us through an uncertain

future, one likely to be marked by grave concerns for the very survival of our species and our planet. So our return to Kabbalah
must be seen in this broader universal context. We are not *just*
Jews coming back to the deep heart of Judaism. We are also
human beings turning to ancient traditions of inner wisdom. We
should rejoice at being part of a worldwide phenomenon, a Jewish
version of a process that the Spirit is bringing about within all the
traditions. As we have much to teach the world from our own
mystical wisdom tradition, we should also be open, more than in
previous times, to learning from others. This is part of the demand of the hour in which we live.

As we have already seen, Kabbalah shows us how deeply all
levels of being are linked to one another. For the kabbalist, God
and world, cosmic macrocosm and each individual human microcosm, all reflect the same structure. This "great chain of Being"
approach to spirituality can be appreciated more than ever by
post-moderns, not only for its beauty, but for a certain dimly perceived accuracy as well. Each human being contains the entire
universe, claims the ancient myth. All the rungs of descent (and
potential ascent) are contained in each soul. This is true even in
a totally demythologized, biological form: all of our ancestors,
each stage and mini-step in the evolution of life that brought us
to where we are today are present within us. The DNA that constitutes the life-identity of each of us exists indeed *zekher le-
ma'aseh bereshit*, "as a memory of the act of Creation," linking us
back to our most remote origins.

Part of our work as self-aware, articulate beings is converting
that biological "memory" into consciousness and building a holy
structure (i.e., a religion or a civilization) that articulates and
sanctifies those links between all generations. In this way, the actual fact of all of our past's presence within us is converted into
a basis for meaning, for expression of our deep rootedness in all
that is and has come before us. The memory of the entire universe
lies within us, and the values represented by that ongoing project

of civilization-building will lead us forward as well, helping us realize that we must be faithful transmitters to all of the many future links in the evolutionary chain, just as we are the grateful recipients of the efforts of all of those who have fought the ongoing life struggle to bring us to this moment. All of the upper and lower worlds of the kabbalist here become manifest in human terms, as generations that lie before and behind us, but also as multiple layers of human self-awareness that we seek to peel back in search of our deepest and truest selves.

OUR TALE OF ORIGINS

A Kabbalah for the future must deal honestly and seriously with our remotest past. How did we all get here? What is the origin of our universe, and how does it fit into a contemporary mystical religion?

In order to examine this question, we must take our inquiry beyond Kabbalah, all the way back to the biblical tale of origins. The question of Creation, a topic mostly ignored in the Jewish theology of the twentieth century, has to be brought back to the forefront. The kabbalists' universe depends entirely on the much older biblical Creation tale, the ingenious opening chapter of Genesis that for nearly 2,500 years served as the chief source for the West's understanding of natural, including human, origins. The account of how God, in six days, spoke each order of existence into being is now of only antiquarian interest as an actual account of how the world came to be, though it remains alive for us as a liturgical text and a source of mythic creativity.

I would like to lift the veil behind the first chapter of Genesis and ask just what it was that this magnificently penned single chapter managed to accomplish. The old Mesopotamian and Canaanite Creation myths, now barely recalled, were well-known to the biblical authors. They include the rising up of the primal forces of chaos, represented chiefly by Yam or Tiamat, gods of the sea, against the order being imposed by the sky gods. The defeat of that primordial rebellion and its bloody end is well documented, as scholars have shown, in a number of passages within the Bible: in the prophets, Psalms, Job, and by subtle implication even in the Genesis text itself. That tale of origins was a part of the cultural legacy of the ancient Israelites. The fact that it is reflected even in post-biblical midrashic sources shows that it had a long life, continuing even into the *Zohar*, of the thirteenth century. The original readers/hearers of Genesis 1, in other words, knew of another account of Creation, one of conflict, slaughter, and victory—"the survival of the fittest" among the gods. What is striking about this account is precisely the absence of those elements of conflict: Genesis 1 offers a purely harmonistic version of the origin of creatures, one where everything has its place as the willed creation of a single deity and all conflict has mysteriously been forgotten.

Our civilization has been transformed over the past century and a half in no small part by our acceptance of a new tale of origins, one that more or less began with Darwin and is refined daily by the work of life scientists and physicists, the new kabbalists of our age who claim even to know the black hole out of which being itself came to be, speculating on the first few seconds of existence as some of the mystics once did on the highest triad of the ten *sefirot*. The history of living creatures is again depicted as a bloody and violent struggle, the implications of which for human behavior—even for the possibilities of human ethics—have hardly gone unnoticed. We, too, are urgently in need of a new and powerfully harmonistic vision, one that will allow even the weakest and most threatened of creatures a legitimate place in this world and protection from being wiped out at the careless whim of the creature who stands, for now, at the top of the evolutionary mound of corpses.

Let us return for a moment to the old Creation tale. While I no longer believe it in any literal sense and do not look to it, even through reinterpretation (each "day" is a geologic era, etc.) as a source of information about geo-history, I claim it still as a religious text that has great meaning for me as a Jew and for us as a people. We still read it in synagogue and its closing section is the introductory rubric for our most precious and best-beloved sacred form: the observance of Shabbat. "Heaven and earth were finished, and all their hosts" (Gen. 2:1). What, then, does the text mean to us? What underlies the myth, or what truth or value are we implying by so privileging this ancient text?

The text says that before there were many, there was only the One. Before the incredible variety and richness of life as we know it could come to be, there had to exist a simple Self, a source from which all the many proceeded. I refer not to some single-celled amoeba that existed in the ocean hundreds of millions of years ago. I refer to a single Being that is the source of the whole evolutionary process, the Source out of which existence has flowed and ever continues to flow.

THE EVER-EVOLVING ONE

This One, I believe, is the only Being that ever was, is, or will be. It is the One that undergoes the only sacred drama that really matters: the bio-history of the universe. I believe that it does so as a conscious and willful Self. From those first seconds of existence, through the emergence of life in its earliest manifestations, and along every step, including the seeming stumblings, missteps, and blind alleys along the way of evolution, it is this single Being that is evolving, entering into each new life form, carrying within itself the memory of all of its past and striving ever onward toward its future. The evolutionary process is here to be re-visioned not as the struggle of creature against creature and species against species, but as the emergence of a single life energy, a single cosmic Mind that uses the comparative adaptabilities of all the forms it enters as a means of going forward into richer and more diverse forms of life. The formless Self, which we call in Hebrew H-W-Y-H, searches out endless forms, delighting to rediscover its own identity anew in each of them. This constant movement of the One, expansive in all directions at once, is at the same time directed movement, pointing toward the eventual emergence of a life form of fully realized self-consciousness. This Being, still in our evolutionary future, will fully know and realize the One that lives in all beings. This creature, the one in whom the self-knowledge of Being can be ultimately fulfilled, is thus the *telos* of existence.

Why do I insist on the conscious willfulness of Creation? It is not just to rescue a noble old religious tradition, one that cannot work without divine purpose. Nor is my goal to save us from facing the absurdity and emptiness of human existence in the face of evolution without purpose. It is rather that I see reality as the mystics do, transcending all changes over time. The consciousness that is present at the end of the process, in the one who comprehends it all (the messianic mind, if you will), is there equally at the beginning of the process. How can the One that contains all, including all of mind and will, be itself lacking them? This is not an argument from divine perfection ("God can do no wrong"), but from the wholeness of Being (the One—or "God"— encompasses all that is). The One exists in a dimension beyond time.

In seeing this One as the source that lies behind the many, I thus understand that the primacy of the One to the many is not necessarily temporal in meaning. To say that the many evolved from the One may be another way of saying "the One created the many." But *both* of these may be too simplistic, too bound to a linear sense of time. One is the ancient myth of Jewish and Christian society; the other may be the new myth of modern Western progressivist society. Myth describes a deep and ineffable reality, one so profound that it is not given to expression except through the veil of narration, through encapsulation in a story. Stories, given the need for a sequential plot, require time. So the precedence of the One over the many, placed into story form, comes out sounding like, "In the beginning God created..." Or it may come forth in modern garb in the narrative of evolution. Its true meaning, however, is that the One underlies the many: then, now, and forever. A dimly perceived but awesome deep structure links all things and ties them to the root from which they all emerge. Multiplicity is the garbing of the One in the coat-of-many-colors existence, the transformation of Y-H-W-H, singularity itself, Being, into the infinite varieties of H-W-Y-H, Being as we know, encounter, and *are* it.

The Genesis Creation story is thus to be read as a tale of the origins of multiplicity, a biblical attempt to answer the eternal question of mystics that the later account of the *sefirot* also addressed: "How do the many proceed from the One?" This reality is symbolized by the fact that Torah begins with the letter *bet*, long a subject of speculation within Jewish tradition. *Bet* is numerically "two"; its positioning at the beginning of Torah indicates that here is the beginning of duality. From this point on, there is not just "God," but "God and..." This meaning is dramatically reinforced by the emergence of Creation in what are repeatedly described as pairs: light and darkness, day and night, heaven and earth, upper and lower waters, sun and moon, male and female, and all the rest. Behind all these twos, however, behind the *bet* of *bereshit bara'* ("In the beginning God created"), lies the hidden, singular, silent *aleph*. This One, representing the absolute Oneness of being, the One after which there can be no "two," is to be proclaimed at Sinai in the opening letter of *anokhi*, "I am," the opening word of the first commandment and the very heart of revelation.

Evolution, too, is an account of the emergence of multiplicity. The divergence of species from one another, the decline of some species and the flourishing of others, and the mechanisms to explain these processes stand at the heart of evolutionary theory. The unity of all species, the shared life energy that flows within them and links them to common ancestry and common sources of nourishment is a factor too abstract and elusive to be the subject of scientific observation or description. This is the point at which science and religion should be seen to complement one another, rather than to stand in conflict. Yes, religion will pull harder in the direction of consciousness and will in its understanding of the evolutionary process; this is its legacy and natural inclination. Science will be more mechanistic and less sweeping in its vision, more inclined to attribute existence to serendipity than to plan. Its own rules forbid conclusions that by their very nature escape verifiable demonstration. Somewhere, in a formula not yet articulated, there lies a meeting of these views, two observations of the same reality.

In the ongoing process of evolution, the emergence of humanity, with its gifts of intellect, self-awareness, and language, is indeed a major step forward. Judaism has always taught a distinction between humans and other forms of life, a sense that the human stands beyond the vegetative and animal realms out of which we emerged. Each creature embodies the life energy and hence the presence of the One, but only humans are called "God's image" in our tradition. This means that we are the first to have the mental capacity to recapitulate the process, to be self-conscious about our roots within the One. The precise implications of that potential can indeed be debated, but surely I do not mean to say that being in the divine image gives us license for the rapacious destruction of all so-called lower forms. God forbid! Of the options provided within the Bible for defining humanity's role, I much prefer Psalm 148's vision of us as *part* of the universal chorus of praise over Genesis 1's isolating us as the final creation on the eve of the Sabbath, with its accompanying message of "stewardship." A true understanding of the unitive vision that is proclaimed here would lead us beyond the demands of "stewardship," the ethic usually derived from the biblical tale. Life's meaning is to be found in discovering the One, and that leads us to realize the ultimate unity of all being. It is in *yiḥud,* discovering and proclaiming the underlying Oneness of all existence, that our humanity is fulfilled.

RECOGNIZING THE SINGLE TRUTH

We are of the One; each human mind is a microcosm, a miniature replica of the single Mind that conceives and becomes the universe. To know that Oneness and recognize it in all our fellow beings is what life is all about. This recognition leads us to another level of awareness. The One *delights* in each of the infinite forms in which it is manifest. To play on that lovely English verb, this means that the One sends its light into each of these forms. Vegetative forms indeed experience this gift most in sunlight, stretching toward it as they grow. We humans are privileged to experience that same radiating light-energy as delight or love.

The One *loves* the many. The coat-of-many-colors in which Being comes to be garbed is a garment of delight. We, as the self-conscious expression of Being, are called upon to love as well, to partake in and give human expression to the delightfulness of existence. This is expressed in Jewish liturgy in the order of daily blessings in our morning prayers. The blessing of God as the source of nature's light is directly followed by a blessing of gratitude for God's love. The One does nothing different in the interim between these blessings. It shines in delight at the eternal procession of "creatures" it comes to inhabit. Nature experiences this shining as light; we humans receive it as love. As recipients of love, we are called upon (dare I say "commanded?") to love as well.

I am also fully willing to admit that we may be but an early stage in an ongoing evolution of aware beings. Perhaps our period will be looked upon in the distant future by creatures who, in discussing a primitive life stage, will be no more willing to demean themselves by the word "human" than we are comfortable being called "ape." Surely they will not be wrong, those wise beings of the future, in seeing our age as characterized by nothing so much as pretentiousness and self-glorification on the one hand and wanton overconsumption and pillage of earth's resources on the other. Let us hope we leave room for that wise future to emerge.

Discovering the presence of the One within the natural order and therefore the sacred quality of existence itself is exactly what our father Abraham did, according to Philo of Alexandria, the first and one of the most profound of all Jewish philosophers. This One manifested itself to him in terms of law: Abraham felt that he was being taught how to live in harmony with the forces of nature. Moses' Torah, according to Philo, is an attempt to legislate for an entire human community the life of harmonic insight with the God of nature that Abraham had already found for himself. I have tried to show elsewhere that certain writings of the Hasidic masters, who were unaware of the ancient precedent, continue this trend.[1] Levi Yizhak of Berdichev, the eighteenth-century Hasidic master, introduces his treatise on hidden miracles, or the miraculous within nature, with precisely this claim: Sinai allows the entire people to apprehend that which wise old Abraham had already long earlier discerned on his own.

AN ENVIRONMENTAL HALAKHAH FOR TOMORROW

The law that teaches us how to live in harmony with the natural world should be one of eternal principles and countless new applications. Its most basic teachings should demand of us that we live at the cutting edge of sensitivity toward the suffering we cause God's creatures. We need be aware of the rest and reinvigoration that we give to the soil, the waste of living resources, for each is the embodiment of the Divine Presence. We may not take the endless material gifts with which we are blessed any more casually than we would take God's name in vain. We may not take the One's great gift of holy water in vain. Or air, source of *nish-mat kol ḥai,* the sacred breath of life. To rest on the laurels of forms our ancestors created long ago or to boast of their progressivism in the tenth or sixth century B.C.E. is very much not to the point. The Torah worked within the cultural limitations of its day to push a new society toward greater humanity and compassion. It even accepted slavery, but tried to put limits on a master's conduct with regard to slaves. We need to catch the momentum of Torah's intent and build on it rather than fall back on it. Starting from the cultural norms of our day, we need to ask: What does the Torah's sensibility demand of us now? How does it seek to push us forward?

Too much of our communal religious energy is devoted to singing the praises of our glorious past rather than facing the challenge of the present hour. What is the point of observing *shemitah,* the sabbatical year that gives rest to the land, while using earth-destroying pesticides? How can we insist on the humanity of *sheḥitah,* kosher slaughter, while we tolerate the hoisting and shackling of animals and the refusal to stun them so as to lessen their awareness before they die? How can carefully pious Jews who take care to wash the bugs out of lettuce to make it kosher go on investing that other green stuff in multinational corporations that daily destroy entire forests? If our commitment to Torah is not merely antiquarian, we need to hear in it a contemporary challenge. How can we *today* create a civilization and a law that will be a *torat ḥayyim,* a teaching that enhances life? And what will it demand of us? Surely a return to the reverence for air, water, and soil would be a good place to start. The new halakhic demands in each of these areas are well known to us. We have only to codify them and commit ourselves to them, as individuals and as a Jewish community.

Perhaps a new mystical theology will seem an awfully convoluted way to get to environmental awareness, especially to readers of a more scientific bent of mind. The language of

Judaism, belonging as it does to such a small segment of humanity, may appear obscure and irrelevant to those most keenly aware
of the immediate threats to global existence. Let me assure you
that I share that sense of urgency. Life has so evolved that the fate
of the biosphere itself is now determined by human actions. We
are masters not only over our own species but also over those we
consume, as so many others have been. The very existence of our
planet as a fit habitat for any living thing has now fallen into
human hands.

With this increase in human power comes a manifold increase
of responsibility. It is the future not only of our own offspring that
we threaten each day with a million decisions weighted with political, economic, and competitive baggage. The land itself, the
adamah from which we humans derive our name, is threatened
by us, the earth and all that is upon it. The changes needed in collective human behavior in order to save us from self-destruction
are stupendous. Belief in their possibility stretches our credulity
as much as it is demanded by our need for hope. Our economic
system, including the value we place on constant expansion and
growth, will have to change. The standards of consumption, created by our wealthiest economies and now the goal of all others,
will have to be diminished. Effective world government, perhaps
even at the cost of some of our precious freedoms, will have to
triumph over the childish bickerings and threats that currently
characterize world affairs.

Hardly believable, indeed, but consider the alternative. If any
of this deep-seated change is to come about, religious leaders and
thinkers need to take an early lead. A seismic shift in the mythi-
cal underpinnings of our consciousness is required; nothing less
will do the trick. This shift will have to come about within the
framework of the religious languages now spoken by large sections of the human race. Experience tells us that newly created
myths do not readily take hold; they usually lack the power to
withstand great challenge. But a rerouting of ancient symbols,

along channels already half-cleared by the most open-eyed thinkers of earlier centuries, might indeed enable this conversion of the human heart of which we speak.

In the emergence of a new tale of origins, we Jews, who have for so long been bearers of the old tale, have a special interest. The new tale will need to achieve its own harmony, summarized with no less genius than was possessed by the author of Genesis 1. It will need to tell of the unity of all beings and help us to feel that fellow creaturehood with trees and rivers, as well as with animals and humans. As it brings us to awareness of our common Source, everpresent in each of us, so must it value the distinctiveness and sacred integrity of each creature on its own, even the animals, or fish, or plants we eat, even the trees we cut down. If we Jews are allowed to have a hand in it, it will also speak of a human dignity that still must be shared with most of our species and of a time of rest, periodic liberation from the treadmill of our struggle for existence in which we can contemplate and enjoy our fellow-feeling with all that is. This sacred time also serves as a model for the world "that is all Sabbath," one that we believe with perfect faith is still to come, a world of which we have never ceased to dream.

9

All about Being Human: Image, Likeness, Memory

YOU *ARE* GOD'S IMAGE

O F THE MANY GIFTS I have been given in the course of my forty-year journey, none has been so important to me as that of great teachers. I have been privileged to learn from some of the finest Jewish thinkers and scholars of the past century, including the friend and teacher to whom this book is dedicated. Not comfortable in the role of disciple to any one teacher, I was able to learn from many, and I am grateful for them all. Among my most important teachers was Abraham Joshua Heschel, theologian and scholar, Hasidic rebbe and prophetic witness. I first read Heschel's writings when I was quite young, and they provided the first intellectual framework for my strong attraction to traditional Judaism. As a rabbinical student, I studied privately with this great master over a period of four years. Ever since, I have been teaching Heschel's writings, recommending them to others, and occasionally writing and lecturing about his work. While I have parted company with his teachings in some aspects of both theory and practice, I continue to see myself as his student.

Although he would never have used the term about himself, I think of Heschel as a *religious humanist*. By that I mean that he believed fully in both the indescribable greatness of God and the potential greatness of human beings. He loved God and he loved humanity, understanding quite fully that love of God had to be expressed by compassion for God's creatures, especially human beings. He also fully understood the awesomeness of human responsibility for the fate of our world. When confronted with the inevitable theological question of the post-Holocaust years— "Where was God?"—Heschel tended to answer with a serious and poignant, "Where was man?" His first book, a collection of Yiddish poems, was called *The Ineffable Name: Man.*[1] Despite his turn from poetry to theology as a medium of expression, along with the forced move from Europe to America and the shift from Yiddish (via German and Hebrew) to English as his language, the value expressed in that title never left him.

From Heschel I learned what it means to live as the image of God. His most important teaching to me, one that stays with me every day, concerns the second of the ten commandments. "Why are we forbidden to make images of God?" Heschel asked. It is not because God is beyond all images, so that no image could possibly depict God. If that were the case, he argued, images would merely be harmless. "God *has* an image," he insisted, "and that is you." You may not *make* the image of God because you *are* the image of God. The only medium in which you can make God's image is the medium of your entire life, and that is precisely what we are commanded to do. Everything you do, everything you say, each moment and the way you use it are all part of the way you build God's image. To take anything less than a full, living human being—like a canvas or a piece of marble—and call it the image of God would be to diminish God, to lessen God's image.

I cannot say that I have succeeded in living each day in accordance with Heschel's teaching. Who could make such a claim? But the teaching has stayed with me, as has the living memory of the one who said it. I, too, have thought long and hard about the verses in Genesis that begin with, "Let us make a human in our form and after our likeness," and have tried to understand how they speak to us in the complicated times in which we live. I also want to see them in the light of a new Kabbalah, one that owes a great debt to Heschel, even though this term—new Kabbalah—is one he would never have used.

The Genesis account begins with two words for what we call "the image of God." *Tselem* is "image" in an almost physical sense, the way in which the child is "the spittin' image" of the parent. The old Aramaic translation (Targum) renders the word by the Greek "icon"; every human being is God's icon. No wonder we have no icons in the synagogue; the synagogue is filled with icons as soon as we walk in! The word *tselem,* by the way, is the basis for the modern Hebrew *matslemah,* the word for "camera," a device than can capture this sort of image. The second term, *demut,* is somewhat more subtle. "Likeness" is probably the right word for it. To be "like" something is to be comparable to it. But here we have a great problem. The prophet says quite clearly, speaking in God's name, "To whom will you compare Me, that I be likened?" and "To whom will you compare God? What likeness can you offer to Him" (Is. 40:18, 25)? Can we indeed be "like" God?

Tselem refers to our hard wiring. We have within us a soul or a spark of inner divinity that is absolutely real and uncompromised. The entire macrocosm, the Self of the universe, is there within each human self, along with the ability, each in our own way, to discover that truth. But *demut* is all about potential. To continue the computer imagery, it is the program we create on the basis of that great hardware, the life we live. We *are* the *tselem* of God; we can choose to become God's *demut* as we work to live and fashion our lives in God's image.

INNER BALANCE: USING THE *SEFIROT*

In our discussion of the ten *sefirot* we saw a good deal of the psychology of Kabbalah. I suggested that the proper balancing of personality, including the struggles to control both anger and perfectionism, is a key message of Kabbalah. In the broader sense, this means that we need to see ourselves as unfinished products, works of God-image still in the making, no matter where we stand in the life cycle. Nothing short of death removes us from this challenge.

Quite a number of years ago, in the late 1970s, I spent a semester teaching in Berkeley, California. Around the corner from our house was (of course!) a spiritual bookstore. In front of the entrance was a huge sign, painted in block letters, that read: "SCIENTOLOGY DOESN'T WORK." Beneath it, in slightly smaller letters, it said something like "INTEGRAL YOGA DOESN'T WORK." And after that, again in smaller letters, "CHRISTIANITY DOESN'T WORK" and "SUFISM DOESN'T WORK." At the bottom of this inverted-pyramid-shaped sign, it said, again in big letters: "*YOU* WORK." Whenever I think of that sign, I am reminded of a saying of the Kotsker rebbe, the toughest of all Hasidic masters. "What does it mean to be a Hasid?" somebody asked him. And he replied, *"Arbetn oif zikh,"* "To work on yourself." Living—making the image of God—is a full-time job.

The work we have to do is partly that of self-control. Keeping a proper lid on *gevurah,* which includes both anger and judgment—the whole harsh and aggressive side of ourselves—is job number one. We are meant to be channels of divine love, conveyers of love and blessing to one another and then back to the Source. *Gevurah* was given to us for balance and containment. It is a necessary tool, but we can't let it run away with us and make us forget why we are here.

While we are on the control side of the ledger, I have to say something about our consumption patterns as well. We live in an age and society of unbelievable luxury, satiety, and creature comfort, when compared with any other human group that has ever lived. Still we are not happy. We want *more:* better health, longer life, cheaper medicine, quieter air conditioners, more channels, fresher sushi, smoother scotch, faster connections to the World Wide Web. Where does it stop? When do I get to ask myself, "Do I really *need* this?" And if I don't, maybe—just maybe—I should do without it. Not because it is wrong, as in "illegal, immoral, or fattening," but because I already consume much more than my share of this world's resources. Maybe I should just let this one go and do without it, whatever "it" happens to be.

We all learn to deal with these issues through our own struggles and each of us comes to terms with them at a different point in our lives. For me it has all been laid out very graphically on the most basic of human consumption issues: food. I've been an overeater since sometime in early childhood, for the usual combination of psychological reasons and physiological proclivities. After many years of up-and-down dieting, in my fifties I found myself getting steadily heavier, even *very* heavy. As I turned sixty, I was getting worried, feeling old and weighted down, even coming to terms with the likelihood of an all too rapidly approaching end. My doctor then convinced me to undergo gastric bypass surgery, a radical treatment for people who need to lose a lot of weight. The surgery was successful. I've lost about a hundred pounds and am in relatively good health.

With the surgery came an interesting life lesson. The weight loss happened because the operation left me with a much smaller active stomach, one that can contain only a small portion of the food I used to eat. Physical hunger contracts to meet the new situation, but psychological hunger, a big part of what we call appetite, does not change so quickly. It is hard to climb out from under fifty years of habit ("of course I'll take a large one"). So here I am, having to ask myself daily, "Do you *really* want to eat that?" Often the answer is, "No, not really." Sometimes I then eat it anyway. As I said, fifty years of habit. The same goes for all our lives as over-consumers. The question, "Do I really need it?" or even, "Do I really want it?" is one we should keep within easy reach.

LEARNING TO FORGIVE OURSELVES

So much for self-control. But all of that is only the more obvious piece of the job. As I said above, we are struggling with our *netzah* as well as our *gevurah*. How do we learn to accept that we cannot do it all, that we will never be quite perfect? How do we learn to forgive ourselves for being mere flawed mortals? Here religion has a great deal to answer for. So often piety has been used to increase people's burdens, wringing out guilt from people whose worst sin was just being human. I have loved the Ba'al Shem Tov for so many years because he understood this. The worst thing you can do, he taught, is to worry too much about your sins. In fact, he said, excessive guilt is the devil's work, the devil's way of keeping you far from God. Only in joy and wholeness can you fully feel God's presence; as long as you are at war with yourself, you have no room in you to make yourself a dwelling place for God.

How do we learn to forgive ourselves? And how do we use religion as a tool for greater self-acceptance rather than self-torment and guilt? Out of the mystical tradition, I believe, the Ba'al Shem Tov learned and taught that you should always keep your eyes on the big picture. We should not let ourselves get too caught up in the details nor let the means become ends in themselves. Despite what is often taught (and misunderstood), Judaism is not all about the details. It's about loving God, sharing that love with God's creatures, making the universe one, and doing it through joy and celebration of life. That's a pretty tall order. So we had better get to it and not let ourselves get distracted on the way. When religion gets in the way of those essential values, instead of being a vehicle to share and express them, it is time to reexamine where we stand.

Rabbi Akiva and his friend Ben Azzai, sometime in the early second century, carried on a wonderful argument. "What is the most basic principle of Torah?" they asked. "What is it all about?" Akiva had a ready answer: "Love your neighbor as yourself" (Lev.19:18). Akiva was Judaism's great advocate for the path of love. For him, the Song of Songs, the love poem of divine or human bridegroom and bride, was the heart of Scripture. The "Holy of Holies," he called it. The tale of the love of Rabbi Akiva and his wife is one of the few truly romantic tales within the rabbinic corpus. So, too, the account of Akiva's death: when he was being tortured to death by the Romans, he supposedly said, "Now I understand the commandment to love God with all your soul— even if He takes your soul." Thus it is no surprise that Akiva is depicted as seeing love to be the most basic rule of Torah.

Ben Azzai disagreed. He said, "On the day when God made human beings, they were made in the likeness of God; male and female God created them" (Gen. 5:1–2) is Torah's most basic principle. Every human being is in God's image, Ben Azzai said to Akiva. Some are easier to love, some are harder. Some days you can love them, some days you cannot. But you still have to treat them all as the image of God. Perhaps Ben Azzai also saw that Akiva's principle might be narrowed, conceived only in terms of your own community. "Your *neighbor*," after all, might refer just to your fellow Jew or your fellow American. How about the stranger? How about the foreign worker in your country? How about your enemy? Ben Azzai's principle leaves no room for exceptions, as it goes back to Creation itself. It's not just "your kind of people" who were created in God's image, but everyone.

Once we have a basic principle, or even a set of basic principles, we have a standard by which to evaluate all other rules and practices, teachings and theological ideas. Does this practice lead us closer to seeing the Divine in every person? Might this interpretation be an obstacle toward doing so? Here lies an inner Jewish basis for raising some important questions, one that should be more in use among those who shape Jewish law for our day. Judaism may indeed exist independently of such extraneous ideas as participatory democracy, egalitarianism, and feminism, but it does not exist separately from its own most basic principle. Any Judaism that veers from the ongoing work of helping us allow every human being to become and be seen as God's image in the fullest way possible is a distortion of Judaism.

To find God in every human being is no small task. We could spend a lifetime attempting to make ourselves perfect and still not be perfect at this one. It's a good thing we have *hod* to balance our *netzaḥ*. A little forgiveness goes a long way, especially when it is ourselves we are forgiving. One thing I have learned along the way is that for many of us—myself, too, on lots of days—the hardest person for us to find God in is ourselves. For this purpose I offer you a favorite teaching by Rabbi Nahman of Bratslav (Hasidic master, 1772–1810), with just a few changes in tone to bring it up to date. Rabbi Nahman was a descendent of the Ba'al Shem Tov and received his legacy of serving God with joy. He was also a person more burdened than most with a sense of sin and guilt. He struggled mightily over these issues, and this teaching is one of the results of that struggle. I study it every year during the month of Elul, preparing for the High Holy Days. I invite you to do the same.

> *You have to judge every person generously.*
>
> *Even if you have reason to think that person is completely wicked,*
>
> *It's your job to look hard and seek out some bit of goodness,*
>
> *Someplace in that person where he is not evil.*
>
> *When you find that bit of goodness*
>
> *And judge the person that way,*
>
> *You may really raise her up to goodness.*
>
> *Treating people this way allows them to be restored,*
>
> *To come to* teshuvah.

This is why the psalmist says:

"Just a little bit more and there will be no wicked one;

You will look at his place and he will not be there" (P. 37:10).

He tells us to judge one and all so generously,

So much on the good side.

Even if we think they're as sinful as can be.

By looking for that "little bit,"

The place, however small, within them where there is no sin

(and everyone, after all, has such a place)

And by telling them, showing them, that that's who they are,

We can help them change their lives.

Even the person you think (and he agrees!) is completely
rotten—

How is it possible that at some time in his life

He has not done some good deed, some mitzvah?

Your job is just to help him look for it, to seek it out,

And then to judge him that way.

Then indeed you will "look at his place"

And find that the wicked one is no longer there—

Not because she has died or disappeared—

But because, with your help, she will no longer be

In the place where you first saw her.

By seeking out that bit of goodness

You allowed her to change,

You helped teshuvah to take its course.

So now, my clever friend,

Now that you know how to treat the wicked

And find some bit of good in them—

Now go do it for yourself as well!

You know what I have taught you:

"Take great care: be happy always!

Stay far, far away from sadness and depression."

I've said it to you more than once.

I know what happens when you start examining yourself.

"No goodness at all," you find. "Just full of sin."

Watch out for Old Man Gloom, my friend,

The one who wants to push you down.

This is one of his best tricks.

That's why I said:

"Now go do it for yourself as well."

You too must have done some good

For someone, sometime.

Now go look for it!

But you find it and discover that it too is full of holes.

You know yourself too well to be fooled:

"Even the good things I did," you say,

"Were all for the wrong reasons.

Impure motives! Lousy deeds!"

Then keep digging, I tell you,

Keep digging,

Because somewhere inside that now tarnished-looking mitzvah,

Somewhere within it there was indeed

A little bit of good.

That's all you need to find:

Just the smallest bit: a dot of goodness.

That should be enough to give you back your life,

To bring you back to joy.

By seeking out that little bit

Even in yourself

And judging yourself that way,

You show yourself that that is who you are.

You can change your whole life this way

And bring yourself to teshuvah.

It's that first little dot of goodness

That's the hardest one to find

(Or the hardest to admit you find!)

The next ones will come a little easier,

Each one following another.

And you know what?

These little dots of goodness in yourself—

After a while you will find that you can sing them!

Join them to one another

And they become your niggun, *your wordless melody.*

You fashion that niggun *by rescuing your own good spirit*

From all that darkness and depression.

The niggun *brings you back to life*

And then you can start to pray...[2]

Rabbi Nahman is talking about self-judgment here, about our most intimate and honest views of our own lives. It is too easy, he warns us, to turn honesty against oneself, to be so brutal in our self-evaluation that we cannot see the good that is there. He is also talking about the soul, the innermost point within the person that is never fully cut off from God, never separated from its Source. The search for the soul and the quest for God cannot be separated from one another. The later Hasidic masters (I think especially of the *Sefat Emet*, whom we have quoted earlier) often spoke of a divine inner point, the "part" of God that lies within the self. This is the object of our inner quest. The point of godliness within has to be discovered, cultivated, and expanded until it becomes the central force around which our lives are shaped.

MEMORY MAKES US HUMAN

Thinking about what it means to live in God's image leads me to another aspect of being human, and that is memory. Here we will touch back on the theme of past, present, and future with which we opened this book. To create a Kabbalah for tomorrow does not mean to forget the past.

The treatise *Pirkei Avot*, the wise sayings of the mishnaic masters, contains a strange list:

Ten things were created on Friday, as the sun was setting: the Mouth of the Earth, the Mouth of the Well, the Mouth of the Ass; the rainbow, the manna, the staff, and the worm; the script, the inscription, and the tablets; (some add: the demons and Moses' burial place) and Abraham's ram (and some add: and tongs, which are made with tongs).[3]

If we delete the "some add" additions, we realize that all these last-minute creations have to do with miracles, moments when resort to the supernatural was required in order to help God's children out of an impossible situation. (How good are you at Bible stories? The Mouth of the Earth swallowed up Korah and the rebels against Moses, the Mouth of Miriam's Well provided water in the wilderness, and the Mouth of the Ass kept Balaam from cursing Israel. The rainbow concluded the flood, the manna sustained Israel for forty years, and the worm bored through the stones used to build the Temple, so they would not be cut with a weapon that could make war. Three miracles are devoted to the writing of the ten commandments on the tablets, and the ram replaced Isaac as a sacrifice.)

There has to be a story behind this list. Why were these things created on Friday at sunset? Why not earlier? Why not just as they were needed? Here is my account of how it happened (all in the language of the old Creation story to be sure. You may translate it, if you like, into post-Darwinese). Each day had its own creations, and after each day God said that it was good. On Friday the land animals were scheduled to be created, and indeed they were. Still God felt there was something missing; it could not yet be called "good." So God turned to whomever God turned (a big puzzle, but not our concern right here) and said, "Let us make humans...." But as soon as the first human beings were there, something new and unanticipated happened to God: *history* opened up before the Throne of Glory.

As long as the world had been inhabited only by plants and animals, there was no history. Plants and animals live, reproduce, and die without leaving memory behind, except in their genes. However, as soon as there were humans, all of human history was stretched out for God to see. And there were humans looking back at God, saying "*You* remember the whole thing." You, Lord, are a God of memory. In fact "remember" was a new word for God, for whom what we call past, present, and future are all one, always. Now God looked "ahead" down this unfurled path of human memory and began to see where humans would get into trouble. Wherever possible, some device was created to help them out of trouble; these were the miracles. And if you ask, "Why are there no miracles in our day?" the answer is obvious. The sun set, and God's time to make miracles ran out. Had Creation gone on, God would have violated the first sabbath, and no one would ever have kept it. For the rest of history after Moses, in other words, Shabbat—the ability to step off the treadmill of humdrum existence—is our only miracle.

To be human is to remember. To lose memory is to lose a piece of ourselves. To lose all of memory is one of the great human tragedies; some part (though surely not all) of the divine light within us goes out with loss of memory. We remember our own lives as individuals, and each person's uniqueness develops over time out of the memories that he or she carries. We remember as families, as tribes, nations, and societies as well. Civilization is built on the passing down, celebration, and interpretation of memory. Rabbi Nahman of Bratslav, in one of his famous *Tales*, asks, "Who remembers the oldest thing?" One of the speakers in the story remembers infancy, another recalls being in the womb, still another remembers the moment of his own (or the world's) conception. But the youngest of the company, who was also the greatest rememberer of all, says, "I remember nothing." This, of course, is the great Nothing that precedes Creation. "And all agreed," Rabbi Nahman concludes, "that this memory was indeed the greatest."[4]

We Jews are *commanded* to remember. We believe that all humans share the command to remember Creation and the covenant with Noah, of which we are all a part. The covenant is God's promise not to destroy the world. The memory of Creation must be our promise to do the same. Today it is we, and not the blind forces of nature, that are the more likely enemies of the world's survival. To remember Creation is to remember that we are here for a purpose: to become aware. We are here to know, articulate, celebrate, and share with all others the truth that Being is One, that H-W-Y-H is Y-H-W-H, that there is none other.

OUR HUMAN TASK: TO *RE-MEMBER*

Here we can turn from the old Creation story to the new one, the sacred version of the tale of evolution that is just beginning to emerge in our day. If the evolutionary process is the ongoing struggle of the Divine One toward intelligent and articulate life forms, as I have suggested, we need to ask ourselves what it is that the One within us needs from us. Why are we here, we creatures who have begun to have some inkling of the process and of the One within it? The answer is that we are here to *re-member*, or to rejoin the links of a creation that have been rent asunder. The job of each human being is to teach every other human being that we are all One, and to find ways in our behavior as well as our thought to include all other creatures within that vision of Oneness as well.

This is the basis of all religion. Judaism teaches us that there are two kinds of commandments: those "between person and God," referring to the spiritual and ritual paths, and those "between person and person," encompassing the moral/ethical life. Both of these categories, I believe, may be seen as rooted in the universal and natural mysticism I am suggesting here. We exist in order to become aware, to lend self-articulation to the One. This, if you will, is the first commandment of nature. It is also the first commandment of Sinai, or at least of its opening words, "I am Y-H-W-H your God." All the rest of religion, insofar as it applies to the realm "between person and God" is just a spelling out of this, a creation of forms through which we remember the single truth. The forms themselves vary from one religion to another, but ultimately they are all arbitrary. We change or restrict our behavior in a certain way, we say certain words or undertake certain actions in order to remind ourselves, on a regular basis, of the truth of God and the Oneness of all being. In this sense we must admit that all of the forms are of human origin; it is people and societies that create or evolve religions. Nevertheless, all of these forms are created as a way of responding to an inner, almost instinctual, drive to recall that deeper truth. In this sense all of the forms are of divine origin, and in this very abstract way we may say that a divine imperative stands behind them.

Our second job as religious people is to share this realization of Oneness with others. We do so most successfully not by preaching, but by actions. We let others know that we and they are part of the same One when we treat them like sisters and brothers, or like parts of our same single universal body. "Love your neighbor as yourself," interpreted to include *all* of our neighbors, is indeed a good "basic principle of Torah." Here all the commandments "between person and person" have their natural root. And here, too, the forms of sharing are based on human experience and methods of social interaction that are wholly ours, yet the imperative that lies behind them derives from a deeper place. We are called upon to proclaim the Oneness of being throughout the world and to enable all those with whom we come in contact to feel themselves to be part of that Oneness as well. Further, we might think about how to extend that sense of "neighbor" beyond the human to the rest of our fellow creatures.

As Jews, we have some other things we have to remember. "Remember that you were a slave in the Land of Egypt" (Deut. 5:15), we are taught; and also, "Remember the day you came out of Egypt, all the days of your life" (Deut. 16:3). Both slavery and liberation must be remembered. These are an essential part of our Jewish vision of being human. Why? The memory of being slaves is our way of identifying with human suffering, especially the suffering of the oppressed. The Torah tells us to remember slavery when it instructs us on how to treat the stranger who lives in our midst. Recalling that we were slaves should make it impossible for us to enslave or oppress others; to do so is a betrayal of our own worst nightmares. To remember the liberation from Egypt is to recall the struggle to become free. We must remember that Pharaoh made things worse once we became troublemakers; we must also remember that we did not leave Egypt empty-handed, but loaded down with gold and silver vessels that had belonged to our oppressors.

All of these memories serve to help us when we look upon others' struggles for freedom from bondage and are called upon to help. They served us in the early days of America's Civil Rights struggles and in the battle for change in South Africa. Of course,

some Jews resisted identifying with the causes of others, thinking of the Exodus as our own exclusive story, but the narrowness
of this reading of Torah was obvious to most. At other times,
however, the message of remembering Egypt becomes much
harder to hear.

I write these words (in Jerusalem, as it happens) in the midst
of a terrible time within Jewish history, a period when we, the
Jewish people, are involved in the oppression of another people,
the Palestinian Arabs who dwell in the Land of Israel together
with us. This book is not a political treatise and I will not pretend
in it to have the answer to one of the most vexing political conflicts of our time. Nor do I in any way seek to diminish the
Palestinian leaders' and people's responsibility for the terrible
atrocities they continue to commit. Some claim that the conquest
of 1967 and the ensuing occupation was forced upon us by
Palestinian intransigence, and was a requirement of self-
preservation. Perhaps it was, but it should have been resolved by
a truly generous solution long ago. Our complicity in the ongoing long-term occupation and settlement remains great, especially as we have profited so much from it. However complex the
genesis of this situation, there is a terrible incongruity of our people's returning to the Land of our ancient freedom, the place
where we came after we ceased to be slaves, only to find ourselves ruling over others in order to keep them from destroying
us. Judaism, as a teaching that demands human freedom, cannot
thrive in such a context. I fear to say that all of us Jews, as well as
the rich Jewish expression that has flourished in the years since
conquest and occupation, will have to struggle long and hard to
free ourselves of the taint of 'oshek, ill-gotten gain attained
through the oppression of others.

Remember slavery and remember liberation. Let them give
you a bad conscience. Sometimes you need it.

The memories of Egypt and of the Exodus are part of our individual spiritual lives as well as our collective heritage as Jews.

They help us to fight our own personal struggles for freedom and give us hope that we can defeat whatever it is that enslaves us, defeat it so fully and finally that we can see it sinking in the deep waters of the sea as we walk across to freedom. The kabbalists say that the divine power that saved us from Egypt was the force of *binah*. *Binah* represents the great mother figure within God, the womb of rebirth. Israel comes forth reborn after crossing the sea; liberation is like a new birth. This is our Jewish way of saying that you can be "born again." It is a vital (in the literal sense of "life-giving") message to all of those who are caught up in the throes of enslavement to compulsive behavior, to addictions, or to whatever it is that leads to slavery or degradation of self. Freedom is a real possibility. The day may yet come when we will dance at the far shore of that sea.

Even that is not the end of the story, to be sure. Forty years of wandering in the wilderness still lie ahead after we come out of Egypt. Sometimes we even think we want to go back. For those moments, my favorite verse of Scripture is, "Just as You have carried this people from Egypt to here..." (Num. 14:19)—when things get bad, we only have to remember how far we have come. The God-given strength that has carried us this far through our wanderings can surely take us the rest of the way as well. Just remember.

10

What about Evil?

REMEMBERING AMALEK, FACING EVIL

J EWS HAVE OTHER MEMORIES AS WELL, not all of them so good
or uplifting. We are commanded to remember what the nation
of Amalek did to us on the way out of Egypt, the way they attacked
the rear of our lines and killed off the weakest and most defense-
less among us. Unfortunately, too much of Jewish history has
confirmed and underscored such memories. A sense of victim-
hood, real or potential, seems to accompany Jewish identity. In
our days, this is linked inevitably to memory of the Holocaust, an
all-too-real event that becomes a symbolic link for us to the entire legacy of Jewish suffering. More than half a century has
passed since the end of Hitler's war against the Jews, but the
wounds are still far from healed. Every threat to Jews, most re-
cently in the form of terror attacks by Palestinians, inevitably
stimulates that memory, even for those of us who know well, in
the rational parts of our minds, to distinguish between one historical situation and another.

To be a Jew is to think about evil. The fact that we have so long
been its victims does not mean that we are never its perpetrators.

It does mean, however, that we live in a universe where the attempt to understand evil and to contend with it cannot be avoided. A return to the Jewish mystical tradition demands some special effort in this regard. The renewed interest in mysticism and spirituality in our times often faces the charge of indifference to human suffering and unwillingness to confront evil. The fear is that mysticism is solipsistic, sinking the person into private inner experience precisely so that the social realities in which we live, with all the responsibility they demand, can be ignored or even forgotten.

Let it first be said that this claim, based on a Western stereotype of Eastern religious values, has little to do with Kabbalah as it has existed in Jewish history. The classical kabbalist saw himself precisely as an actor on the cosmic stage, battling the powers of evil and defending *shekhinah* against their wicked designs. Mystical intentionality combined with the divine power inherent in the commandments to make the kabbalist a powerful actor in the struggle between good and evil forces. The *Zohar* depicts the *tzaddik* as a kind of spiritual knight in armor, standing guard against those demonic powers that so often seem to rule this world. Activism and mysticism were fully integrated in the self-image of those who created Kabbalah.

Our view, both of ourselves and of our own mysticism, is somewhat different. The classical kabbalists believed in the theurgic or transformative power of human actions. By performing the *mitzvot* with proper understanding and devotion, they saw themselves as giving strength to God, arousing the divine energies in such a way that good would triumph and evil would be defeated. God's active presence would enter this world depending on the quotient of spiritual power mustered by those who directed their will toward this effort.

The difference between this view and that of contemporary Jewish mysticism is subtle but significant. For us, there is nothing magical in the power of the commandments. Yes, we too believe that we add to the positive energy quotient in the cosmos by the gift of our devotion. This gift may be borne by a specific *mitzvah* or by any deed offered in love and awe, as the Hasidic masters have taught us. But the good that comes of such acts is seen in more modest and realistic terms, measured chiefly in their effects on our own lives and the ways in which we relate to those around us.

This means that commandments and transgressions of Torah are no longer identified with the cosmic forces of good and evil, as they once were. The great battle against the demonic, so much a part of Kabbalah, especially on the popular level, is not what we have in mind. Our demons are chiefly internal, and we see them more as psychological weaknesses or obstacles than as conscious and active forces of destruction. Still, in proposing a contemporary Jewish mysticism, we must address the problem of evil. The terms in which the existence of evil are problematic will differ here from the classical formulations of most Western theology, just as mystical religion, with its tendency toward monism, differs from classic theism. More importantly, we want to discuss this issue not as a theoretical abstraction but from a place of deep compassion for human suffering, and a commitment both to relieve the pain of those around us and to stand up in the face of real evil when we are called upon to do so.

THE PROBLEM OF SUFFERING

Let us turn first to the question of suffering, which is not the same as that of evil, but is often confused with it. A key test to apply to any theology is to see if it rings true in the presence of human suffering. That is not to say, as do the Buddhists, that suffering is *the* universal human condition. Judaism knows and recognizes human suffering, but does not see it as constant. Moments of joy, love, and fulfillment are no less part of human life than those of pain and devastation. All of these are equally both real and unreal.

Suffering comes to us through any number of causes. Many of them are simply the result of nature: disease, aging, and natural disasters. All of these take a tremendous toll in human pain. Every day young people are afflicted by terrible illnesses; innocent people are drowned, buried alive in earthquakes and avalanches, fall off cliffs, or get lost in deserts. All of these possibilities horrify and frighten us. They are sad, even tragic. But they are not *evil.* While our outcry against the seeming injustice of such sufferings is to be expected, there is no one to blame, and we know it. To be an adult is to understand that we are mortal and that life is not fair. None of us is immune to disaster.

Perhaps as much suffering occurs due to human actions that are undertaken without malice. We do things to ourselves that destroy our own health and well-being, leading to great pain and sometimes to death. And we do things to others, without the intention to harm. Accidents and mishaps of various kinds occur throughout human life, and these too may be causes of suffering.

What does a contemporary mystical faith have to say in the face of human suffering? First, it does not seek to provide an "answer" that will try to explain suffering and make it disappear. It does not claim that suffering is unreal. Nor does it say that the one who suffers must be unworthy and deserving of the fate received. We must always be careful not to blame the victims, as the guilt feelings fostered and buttressed by religion have so often done.

God is everywhere. The One that underlies all being is to be found in moments of pain as well as times of joy. God is present in places of devastation as well as where there is joy, in the house of mourning as well as the house of feasting. We may both seek and find the face of God wherever we are, even in the pain of great loss. While we should never look for suffering in order to find God in it, many say that they first came to a deeper spiritual consciousness in confronting terrible pain or loss.

What does it mean to "find God" in a moment of suffering? To find God is to change perspective, even when the reality of suffering itself cannot be changed. It is to allow a chance for the deep force of healing that comes from a level of consciousness beyond our control or knowledge to work its magic on us. This healing may take the form of accepting what cannot be changed, of coming to terms with a new situation. That in itself can be an important step forward. The kabbalists also teach that one can always *uplevel* a human situation, lifting it to its root within God. In doing so the pain may be sweetened. Previously unseen sparks of light, precious bits of divinity that had been covered over by the pain, may be discovered. As we restore these to their root in the single One, a glimpse of possible transformation may be given to us.

Uplevelling (*ha'ala'ah* in Hebrew) is understood by the kabbalist to mean reflecting the true single nature of the universe. The One underlies the many. The universal Mind of God stands behind each individual human mind and is manifest in it. The great cosmic Heart of all being, the Source of divine love, is present in every feeling and act of love. In turning inward, we open ourselves to deeper levels of consciousness that exist in our minds, inner places where we can be more open to these great truths. We bring our pain with us to those places.

The kabbalist perceives three parallel levels of existence: this world, the inner life of God, and the Mystery beyond all words. A person who suffers has to lift his/her own woes to the level of *shekhinah*. This Divine Presence is in exile, sharing in the pain of all who suffer. The Jews have long pictured *shekhinah* wandering about the world, sharing in the exile of Israel. Of course she is there with every one of her other children as well. "I am with him in sorrow," says the psalmist (91:15), and the Rabbis comment that God participates in human suffering.[1] When we feel this higher presence within us, we also come to see the smallness of our own sorrows, understanding that the more real pain is that of *shekhinah*, the Mother, who takes to herself all of human suffering.

When we come to identify with *shekhinah*, seeing our own pain as a reflection of hers, we open ourselves to discovering a yet higher level, that of *binah,* the source of life to which we all return. *Binah* is a mystery we can't quite know. She represents the fiftieth rung of knowledge, just beyond the forty-nine that we can enter with the fullest effort of our minds. The *Zohar* teaches that *binah* is a question, not an answer. *Binah* is also the deep inner place that suffers no exile, the Self of the universe that remains pristine, undamaged by all that transpires, perfect. This is the ultimate healing force, and its powers are accessible to us.

Like *shekhinah, binah* too is a maternal presence. *Shekhinah* is the Mother who is here with us, sharing in our pains and joys, making them her own. *Binah* is a deeper mother, the womb of existence itself. She is called the great jubilee, because the Torah tells us that in the fiftieth, or jubilee year, "each one will return to the place to which he holds fast, to his own inheritance" (Lev. 25:13). *Binah* is thus the mother who redeems, who takes us out of bondage, who heals our ills. Yes, she may be death, because there is no full return to our source short of death itself; in life we are given only the briefest glimpse into *binah.* But she is also life, the Source of all life, the power of rebirth and renewal. It is because the life-energy of *binah* is never depleted that the kabbalists insist on the possibility that the dead will live again, whether in this body or another, whether now or in a time and place beyond our ken, even beyond imagining. *Binah* must remain a mystery. It is that of which Scripture says, "No eye has seen, O God, but Yours" (Is. 64:3).

EVIL AND HUMAN ORIGINS: TWO TALES

Evil, in contrast to suffering, requires malice. It is the conscious desire of one human being to cause harm to others, or the cruel and wanton indifference to the pain brought upon others as we seek to fulfill some desire of our own. Evil, in other words, is a human creation, the meeting of our clever minds, our selfish desires, and our deepest insecurities. Each human being has the power to attain great heights, to become the image of God. We also have the potential for cruelty and depravity that know no limit, as we have seen so vividly, over and over again, in the course of the past century.

The Bible opens with a pair of tales that describe the origin of evil. The first is that of Adam and Eve, expelled from Eden because they could not resist temptation. Eve saw that the fruit of the Tree of Knowledge was good to eat and her husband was tempted along with her. Hesitating to sin because of God's word, she let herself be convinced by the serpent that God, in prohibiting the fruit of that tree, was only protecting God's own unique position. Anyone who ate of it, the serpent said, would be "like God, knowing good and evil" (Gen. 3:5).

How right the serpent was! Only by eating the fruit could we know what good and evil are. Only by realizing that we have urges we cannot control, temptations we cannot overcome, do we realize the seriousness of our human moral condition. Only once we have stumbled are good and evil set out before us as two diverging paths between which we have to choose at every single step of the way. We *had to* eat of the fruit in order to become adults, in order to live outside the realm of childlike paradise.

A Hasidic tale is told of two pious brothers, Reb Elimelech and Reb Zusya:

> "How can it be," Reb Elimelech asked his brother, "that Adam ate of the fruit? We are taught that the soul of every human ever to be born was there in the soul of Adam. If such a holy soul as yours was there within him, how did you let him eat it?" Rabbi Zusya looked at him with sadness. "Of course I was there," he said, "and I knew how dangerous was the sin. But I also knew that if I stopped him, our situation would be even worse. We would have gone on forever saying, 'If only I had tried it! If only I had eaten!'"[2]

The early kabbalists offer another profound teaching about the tale of Eden. Reading the text closely, they say, shows us that there were two trees at the center of the garden: the Tree of Knowledge and the Tree of Life. These two trees were joined to one another, knowledge and life (or Creation and Revelation, World and Torah), being, in their essence, one. Adam and Eve's sin was plucking the fruit. In doing so, they separated the two trees, tasting only of knowledge, but in such a way that it was cut off from its root in the Tree of Life. Their sin was separation, breaking apart the unity of being. The kabbalists understood the break between the two trees as dividing the *sefirot,* seeking to worship *shekhinah* alone, cut off from her deeper roots within the Godhead.[2] *Shekhinah* is presence, the God of religious experience. In choosing only a God we can experience, while ignoring the mystery beyond, we run the risk of worshiping experience itself, thus turning *shekhinah* into a Golden Calf. Here, the two great sins of the Torah are seen as one. The kabbalists also remind us that we repeat the sin of Eden each time we seek to turn living Torah into mere information. We who spend our lives in universities know all about this separation of knowledge from life. We may be fated to dwell outside of Eden, but Torah must remain our link to the Tree of Life.

Evil begins in the real world with the second human story of Genesis, the tale of Cain and Abel. This is the story of the first human life outside the Garden. Cain offers a sacrifice to God, the fruit of his labors in tilling the soil. Such an offering was his own idea; God had not asked him for it. Abel copied him, but he raised the ante. He offered God a *better* sacrifice, burnt flesh from the best of his flocks. For no apparent reason (except perhaps that God isn't a vegetarian!), God responded to Abel's sacrifice and ignored that of Cain. Furious, dejected, Cain rose up and killed his brother. God demanded an account of him, held him responsible for the killing, and punished him with lifelong exile.

Yes, Cain is guilty. He tried to defend himself, according to the midrash, by saying that murder was not yet forbidden, or even by claiming that he did not know what death was and did not realize that hitting a man with a rock would do such great harm. But God would have none of it. This is what it means to live outside Eden, to be a morally responsible adult. Even if no one tells you what is wrong, you are supposed to know. This is still the basis for prosecuting crimes against humanity in our day. There is a limit to moral relativism: even if your society does not consider it a crime, you are supposed to know.

Why did Cain do it? Frustration, anger, rage, jealousy all come to mind. He is responding to God's arbitrariness, to the seeming injustice of life. *Why* should God ignore his sacrifice? Wasn't he the one to come up with the idea? Is God then *wicked* to disregard his offering? Is Cain the author of the first evil, or is it God? The tale is indeed a challenge to faith. The authors of Genesis showed great daring in placing it as the first story of life outside of Eden.

God cannot really be called the villain of the story. This account of divine indifference is the tale's way of noticing the reality of life that sooner or later confronts us all. There is no answer as to why some seem to be favored by God and prosper, while others, perhaps even more deserving by our best human measures, fail and suffer. Life is just not fair. Perhaps Cain would really have liked to lash out against God in protest, but God was not within reach for attack. Abel was the only available victim for Cain's rage.

THE STRUGGLE AGAINST EVIL: TWO MODELS

What is the source of the deep anger and frustration that we carry with us through our lives? And what are we supposed to do about it? Is life just a constant struggle to control our own worst instincts, or is there a more basic way to overcome them? Judaism seems to offer two models regarding the struggle against evil, one from biblical and rabbinic sources, and the other, while also of ancient origins, more specifically characteristic of Kabbalah. According to the first model, the human being is a *tabula rasa*, a blank slate, or an open field in which the great conflict takes place between two opposing instinctual forces, the good and evil urges. Interestingly, only the evil urge is mentioned in the Bible; Genesis claims that "the inclination of the human heart is evil since youth" (Gen. 6:5; 8:21). The Rabbis sought to equalize the playing field, seeing the two urges in constant struggle with one another. The laws and prohibitions of Torah support the good urge, yet the will to do evil, often identified with ego and libidinal drives, remains very strong.

The second model is that of core and shell. The human being has an inner core, the soul, which is pure and untainted. "Lord, the soul You placed in me is pure," says the daily morning service. Evil arises in the hard shell that surrounds our core, a shell that exists for the purpose of defense and self-preservation. The "real" person is the one inside the shell, but that inner self is sometimes deeply hidden, even from ourselves. Various things that happen to us in life—especially experiences of victimization and hurt to the frail ego of childhood—make us add layers onto the shell, so that it becomes harder, sometimes almost impossible, to ever break through it.

The story of Cain seems to follow the first model in its harsher biblical version. There is no force of good here, only Cain's uncontrollable rage. Another reading of it may be found, however, in the difficult key verse in which God warns Cain, "Sin crouches at the entranceway. Its desire is for you, but you may rule over it" (Gen. 4:7). This seems to be the evil urge, ever ready to spring up and overwhelm the person. The text leaves room, as it so often does, for another interpretation as well. Why does sin crouch "at the entranceway?" The entranceway to what? Some say this is the entranceway to life, another proof that wickedness begins in childhood. Suppose we read it as referring to the entranceway to the innermost self? When does sin—read it as violence, aggression, or rage—arise? It comes up *at the entranceway*. When we try to find our innermost self, the way is blocked. The self within is entirely vulnerable. Having it exposed is too threatening to most of us, most of the time. When faced with the possibility of openness, *la-petah*, at the entranceway, we run desperately in the other direction. Much of the evil that we do comes about in the course of our flight from our own vulnerability.

Cain is still responsible for his actions. So are all the other perpetrators of evil and violence throughout history. To say that Hitler was probably a wounded child is not to excuse his behavior or to lessen his guilt. Our attempt to understand the source of much of that violence by thinking of the threatened core and the building up of the shell is not meant to diminish the full responsibility of sane adults for their evil deeds. It does mean, however, that things could have gone differently. The worst villain started life with a pure and holy soul, the same as the greatest saint. True, each child is unique, and souls differ from one another. But there are no souls that are evil or tainted from birth. Everyone has the potential for a life of holiness. In the way we raise children, in the way we treat our neighbors, our task is to always stand by that child's soul and help it grow into a healthy and unthreatened human personality.

The mystic's response to evil lies in training the self toward greater openness. We must learn to be less afraid, and endeavor to build a society and a vision of humanity less dependent on the thickness of our shells. This is the real work, the worldly task, of those who have been privileged with insight into the spirit. Stripped to its essentials, the real meaning of this book and all my teachings is the message of the open heart. This is the core question: *How do we learn to live in a more openhearted way? How does Judaism serve as a vehicle to lead us to openheartedness?* The job is not made easier when we need to do it, as did the builders of the Second Temple, "with one hand building, while the other hand is holding a weapon" (Neh. 4:11). There is a degree to which defenses are healthy and necessary for survival, especially in a world of real threats and hostilities. Learning to navigate between the need for self-protection and the dangers of our own aggressiveness can be a lifelong task.

GOD AND EVIL

We still have not responded to the *theological* problem of evil. For the conventional Western believer, the question is: Why does a good and all-powerful God *allow* evil to exist? If God rules the universe, why is the force of evil not vanquished? The mystical faith proposed here cannot respond to the question posed in that way, because it is not based on the model of God as providential Actor, the cosmic Ruler who measures out just rewards to the righteous and duly punishes the wicked. Still, our faith in a single unified vision of reality also must struggle with evil. If all of existence is part of God, if H-W-Y-H reflects Y-H-W-H, as we have said it, what is evil doing in it? Is the bleak soul of the child-murderer also part of God? Are hatred and violence just as much reflections of the one Being as love and compassion? Are we willing to worship such a God? And who says that we worship the God of all Being by doing good? Is not evil also an imitation of the One that contains all?

It is clear that we have no easy answers. People of faith have struggled with this question throughout history and will continue to do so long after we are gone. I am suggesting a contemporary version of the kabbalist's way of dealing with this issue, one that may add some new depth and texture to our struggle, rather than serving as a way to dismiss the question.

Indeed there is only One. The one Being who is and underlies all of reality seeks ever to be revealed, to be known by the creatures whose forms it fills, in each of whom it is incarnate. This is the drive behind the whole evolutionary process, the One seeking that form of life that would come to know, love, and articulate it. This process, stretched over millions of years, is not one of a perfect wise Creator who has all the answers, but rather of a spreading life-energy, moved by eternal quest. It engages in that pursuit by the method of trial and error. There have been great blind alleys in evolution, and progress toward higher consciousness has then proceeded in other, more fruitful, directions.

Among the methods used by the life force in this quest is that of violent aggression. Species learn to grow stronger and more clever by fighting, killing, and devouring one another. The struggle for territory, limited resources, and more fruitful mating partners has indeed gone on throughout biohistory. As products of that process, we, too, contain all of those drives within us. They are the source of the "evil urge," representing within the individual what the old kabbalists called "the other side," or the demonic presence within reality. For them, this force originated in a flaw that appeared within the sefirotic universe. As the ten emerged from the One along the road to multiplicity, there had to be a limiting, judging, and ultimately negative force, in order that creatures other than the One might come to exist. I am suggesting an evolutionary version of evil's origin that leads in the same direction. Yes, all is One. But for reasons that were necessary as existence proceeded, that One had to emerge in a way that includes within it the drive toward aggression, the urge to survive and excel, and with them, the potential that in humans manifests itself as evil.

At its root, the One is beyond these drives, and it is to that One that we seek to return. God is the soul of the universe, the pure core of Being, parallel to the soul within each of us. The innermost place within God, as within the soul, is *keter*, the rung of pure compassion. It is that One that we seek; it is to there that we long to return. As humans, creatures who have begun to understand and appreciate the meaning of the great evolutionary struggle, our job is to seek that core within ourselves, in others, and in the cosmos as a whole. This is why we have religions. They offer us tools, linguistic and symbolic guideposts, that help us to engage in our search for the eternal One. They also provide norms and paradigms through which to exercise moral judgments, which, in the first place, are to be exercised in relation to ourselves, helping us to control those aggressive urges that are indeed a vital part of our inner nature or evolutionary legacy, but which nevertheless must be kept in their place as we dare to assert that to be human is different—is indeed to be in the image of God.

The soul within us remains pure; even the greatest sinner, the doer of the most heinous deeds, has a pure soul. To gain access to that unsullied self requires great, sometimes super-human effort. *Teshuvah*, the process of return and transformation, is not to be taken lightly. Perhaps the old kabbalists knew something when they prescribed severe but specific penances for one sin or another: so many days of fasting, so many hours rolling naked in the snow, so many lashes of the whip. We no longer have or seek those defined forms of penance, but their presence in the sources is a good reminder that *teshuvah* does not come easily.

What can we say of the One? Having entered into the process of evolution, allowing for the competition, aggression, and violence that developed as they did, can we assert that the One that lies at the core of all being remains transcendent, pure, and undefiled? To say it in more personified theological language: can the God who, for whatever necessary reasons, permitted evil to exist, even using it as a tool of evolution, remain God? Or must God, too, seek out penance in order to return to an original place of purity? How does God achieve atonement?

The question, so strange to our theological ears, is no surprise to the student of Kabbalah. An ancient Talmudic legend explains the presence of an atonement offering among the sacrifices prescribed for the New Moon, generally seen as a time of feasting. It tells a tale about the sun and the moon, originally created as "the two great lights" (Gen. 1:16).

God then saw that sunlight needed to be stronger, to create the bright light of day, while moonlight should be dim, to faintly illumine the night. "Go diminish yourself," God said to the moon.

When she protested, God had to force her to be smaller, and God made her light to wax and wane each month. But divine justice understood that this was wrong, that God had sinned in retracting the moon's original equality. Life, as God created it, or as it emerged from within the One, is not fair. Therefore, God said that on each new moon day, among Israel's offerings, was the obligation to "bring an atonement for Me, because I diminished the moon."[4]

The kabbalists understand this tale as a profound admission that God has created an imperfect universe, and that a degree of moral responsibility reaches the Creator. Its meaning is extended in various directions: the "diminishing of the moon" as God's sin is applied to the separation of *shekhinah* from the higher *sefirot.* Alienation begins within God; it is an essential part of the bringing forth of the "other." Hence all that follows, including the pain wrought by the soul's sense of distance from God, the universal human state of exile, and all of the violence and evil we bring forth as a result of these, are God's responsibility as well as ours. At the same time, the tale of God's diminishing the moon's light also has a more specific meaning: it contains a strong implication that the inequality of the sexes, as it emerged in the course of human history, is a divine "sin." For all of these God must seek a penance. But that divine atonement can be found only in the course of a relationship with humanity ("...bring an atonement *for* Me..."), just as *our* atonement can be found only in relationship with God. The Rabbis sharply read a verse of Scripture to mean, "the Lord will return *along with* your return" (Deut. 30:3).[5] They understood, as we do ever more sharply today, that the need for *teshuvah* exists on more than just the human plane. We and God both need to return to the original plan, to repent. And we can only do so *together*.

11

The Life of Prayer

CULTIVATING INWARDNESS

WHILE THE ENTIRE RELIGIOUS life is pointed toward the goal of inner awareness, the greatest vehicle our tradition offers for opening the heart is prayer. It is in the moment of prayer and in the course of a life shaped and defined by prayer that we come to know and appreciate our place as Godly creatures and as centers of divine light. We now have to turn to prayer and ask what it means and how can we use it when on this path of spiritual awakening.

Prayer is traditionally divided into two categories. First is spontaneous prayer, words that flow directly from the heart in response to the events of our lives. The Bible is frequent witness to such prayers, ranging from Moses' one-line outcry when his sister was taken ill—"Please, God, heal her!" (Num. 12:13)—to the triumphant Song at the Sea (Ex. 15) or many of the Psalms. Such prayers, whether verbal or silent, belong to a particular moment, and their power lies in the direct expression they give to the pain or joy of that moment.

The second sort of prayer is liturgical or fixed prayer—*tefillat keva'* in Hebrew—assigned words to be spoken regularly at certain times in the day, week, or year. These prayers evoke powerful responses in us precisely because of their familiarity. To recite them regularly is to develop an attachment to their poetic phrases, their melodies, and various meanings we link with them. Each time we recite them, all of our memories of the many other times we said them, along with the recall of prior generations who spoke these same prayers, are there with us. This well of memory creates a deep echo-chamber, lending a richness and profundity to the words of prayer. It is this sort of regular prayer that is especially characteristic of Judaism.

How are we to understand the process of prayer? Precisely what is it that we seek to do when we pray? And how does this fit into the old/new Judaism of mystical awareness that is the theme of this book?

A HASID'S PRAYER

Let us begin with a negative. What is it that prayer does *not* mean? Prayer is not simply a conversation with God, one in which you, the pray-er, are on one side of a conversation and doing the speaking, while God is "somewhere else," and is either listening or not. I like to illustrate this model of prayer, which is unfortunately held by most people, through the story of a Hasid in the telephone booth.

It seems that our friend the Hasid is having a very busy afternoon at his business affairs, running all over New York trying to get things done on time. A little after 6 P.M. (it must be early spring), he is dashing through Grand Central Station and he realizes that he has not yet recited *minḥah*, the afternoon prayer, and the latest time for doing so is fast approaching. A bit too self-conscious to just stand up against a wall in the busy station and begin to pray, he looks up and sees a bay of telephones, several of which are empty. He walks over to the phones, picks one up, and starts to recite his prayers. He begins to pray: "Happy are those who dwell in Your house; they shall forever praise You."

At that moment the great station is God's house, and the Hasid's prayer may be deeply from the heart. It should not be judged by the too-simple question: "Is there anybody on the other end of the line?" The relationship between the one who prays and the One who receives prayer is *not* that of the two ends of the telephone.

Many years ago, a friend and I were preparing a collection of Hasidic teachings on prayer for an English language anthology.[1] The one that stood out above all of the others and has remained closest to my heart is a teaching of Rabbi Pinḥas of Korets, a close friend of the Baʿal Shem Tov. Rabbi Pinḥas said, "People think that you pray *to* God, but that is not the case. Rather prayer itself is of the essence of divinity."[2]

Where is God as our friend begins his prayers with the telephone receiver in his hand? All around him, of course, filling that vast hall just as intensely as the Tabernacle was filled, when there was so much God in it that Moses himself was unable to enter (Ex. 40:35). And God is in our Hasid's heart, just as God is in the hearts of all those other folks standing at the phones, those talking to sick children at home, those listening to the latest stock quotations, and those cursing out their travel agents for messing up the tickets. If we could only see and hear that busy room from the divine point of view, we would be witnessing a New York City afternoon version of the great symphony, a true chorus of the angels! In fact, the only difference between the Hasid and all those around him is that he has stopped to *listen*. He has taken the time to *acknowledge* that he dwells in God's house. God is present in his saying of those words. And, if he is paying attention to the moment, *he* is present as well.

Prayer, then, is about listening as much as it is about speaking. "Let your ear hear what your mouth is saying!" the Rabbis teach regarding the proper way to pray. If "prayer itself is of the essence of divinity," the entire process of prayer is a holy one, taking place inside us and around us. In prayer we give voice to the deepest self that lies hidden within us, the spark of divinity that lies within our soul. That innermost spark, like the highest, primordial Torah, dwells in a realm far beyond words. We give it the gift of language, allowing it to come forth and be present to the world of our conscious selves.

The greatest masters of prayer have always understood that the act of praying is not one we can do alone. A verse from the Psalms—"Lord, open my lips that my mouth may flow with Your praise" (Ps. 51:17)—was placed before the *'amidah*, the main body of prayer in each service, to remind us of this. We do not pray alone. God prays through us! We provide the words; the divine stirring in the depths of our souls makes the music.

On the face of things, prayer is absurd. Do we really need to communicate with God in human language, by moving our mouths and making sounds in our throats? Is this the way to reach the One who knows our hearts, who indeed *is* our deepest heart? Why language? What place is there for words between us?

For prayer to be *ours*, to be a vehicle for the soul or the Divine within to communicate with us, it has to be in our language. Not because God needs words, but because *we* do. It is also important that prayer be in the sort of language that touches us most deeply. As the innermost self, really the Self of God within us, makes itself manifest to us, it must reach and "travel" through all of our most vulnerable and wounded places. To do so, it needs the language that can reach us where we hurt and where we feel true joy.

I do not know much about the power of prayer to affect others: to heal the sick, to bring home the lost, to protect those we love from harm. I remain somewhat neutral to the claims now being made again, on this far side of the age of skepticism, for the efficacy of prayer in the external world. But I know that prayer heals the one who prays, restoring a wholeness or a balance that can be lost when we are beset by concern or worry. This, too, is a great healing, one not to be taken lightly. And since the One who lies within us, to whom we give the words of prayer, lies as well within the heart of the one for whom we pray, we would indeed be setting false and unnecessary limits to say that the energy of our love, expressed in that prayer, *cannot* reach the other.

THE GIFT ON THE INNER ALTAR

The term most Ashkenazic Jews use for traditional prayer is *davnen*, a word that has long puzzled scholars of the Yiddish language. It has no analogue in German, Hebrew, or Slavic languages, the usual sources of Yiddish. Some have tried to connect it to the Latin *divinus*, others to the English word *dawn*. I once heard a famous Yiddish scholar suggest that it originally served as a translation of the Hebrew *minḥah*, and that it derives from a Lithuanian word meaning "gift." He claimed that the Jewish *shtetl* storekeeper, who had to explain that it was time for him to recite afternoon *minḥah* prayers, was the source of this translation into the local language. Be the real etymology whatever it is, I have always liked this idea of *davnen*, or praying as giving a gift.

After the ancient Temple in Jerusalem was destroyed, prayer replaced the sacrifices that had been offered there. Such sacrifices were indeed a gift. It was no small thing for the farmer to bring a prize animal to the Temple. The gift of words seems paltry by comparison, a gift too easily falsified and costing us nothing at all. We should remember what lay behind the sacrificial gift. Animal sacrifice replaced human sacrifice at some early point in ancient history, but the memory of that human sacrifice was never totally forgotten. There was a time in ancient Israel when first-born sons were sacrificed. Both the story of the binding of Isaac and that of the slaying of the Egyptians' first-born bear echoes of that horror. (In Christianity, in fact, it remained crucial to the central act of worship. The sacrifice was offered by God, but the shedding of human blood was still required for atonement.) The offering of a son was itself a substitution; one gave a new life instead of giving one's own. The sense was that we owe our lives to God (or the gods, in earlier times), and God has a right to demand life of us. We ward off that demand, at least for a while, by offering the life of a beloved child.

How distant we are from those ancient memories, and how unchanged is our essential situation! Yes, we still owe our lives to the mysterious force of life that is both within us and far beyond our comprehension or control. We are still mortals who one day will have to let go of life, and we still hope to postpone the coming of that day as best we can. But we do not sacrifice our children. Prayer comes in place of sacrifice. In true prayer, we give the only gift we have to offer: ourselves. *Va-ani tefillati,* says the psalmist (69:14), felicitously mistranslated by later Hasidic readers as "I *am* my prayer."[3] We have learned, though, that to give ourselves to God does not mean to climb up on the altar. The prophets long ago taught us a better way. We give ourselves by opening our hearts, by being present to God's presence in our lives, by sharing with others, by generosity toward the needy, among whom God's spirit rests.

Now we see the cycle of prayer in its wholeness, and we can begin to appreciate the comment of Rabbi Pinhas of Korets that prayer is the essence of divinity. I say, "Lord, open my lips." I ask God for the strength to help me pray, to be present within my prayer. What is it that I ask of God? To help me give myself to God! "Help me, O Lord, to give myself to You!" We seek the God deep within to be present as we offer ourselves to the God beyond, the One who is of course in no way separate from the One within. Indeed "prayer itself is of the essence of divinity."

We have only one more step to go. If I am all I have to give to God, I must allow the same to be true of God as well. All God has to give me is God. The Ba'al Shem Tov read Psalm 102, titled "The Prayer of a Poor Man," as "A Prayer *to* a Poor Man." "Come before God as you would to a poor person," he said. "Do not expect any gifts, any riches."[4] All God has to give you is God's own self. So too did the Hasidic masters read the prophet's words, "Blessed is the person who trusts in Y-H-W-H; Y-H-W-H is the object of their trust" (Jer. 17:7). "Why the seeming repetition in this verse?" they asked. "We truly trust in God," they said, "when all we want of God is God."

THE FUTURE OF JEWISH PRAYER

The transition from sacrificial to verbal worship in Judaism seems as though it was an abrupt one. Suddenly the Temple was destroyed, sacrifices were no more, and prayer replaced them. The process, in fact, was a much longer and more subtle one. Rabbinic prayers were developing a century or more before the Romans sacked Jerusalem and burned down the Temple. And for centuries afterward, even down to the present day, Judaism refused to fully make peace with this transition. The traditional prayerbook, after each 'amidah, still calls upon God to rebuild the Temple so that we can make our proper offering. The *mussaf* ("additional") service for sabbaths and festivals still lists the appropriate sacrifice of the day.

I mention this transition and its slowness because it occurs to me, as it may have to you, that we are at the edge of another such transition in our history. The great interest in meditation and inner silence in our day has attracted many of our most serious seekers. We are learning a great deal about this part of spiritual life from our dialogue with Buddhist and Hindu teachers, but we are also examining lost/forgotten inner Jewish resources on the value of inner silence. More books on the topic of "Jewish meditation" have been written in the past ten years than were written in the prior thousand! We seem to be moving toward an age in which prayer will transcend language, where the silent prayer of the heart will learn to be spoken directly, without the aid of words.

I feel open to this transition and see it as an important part of our Kabbalah for tomorrow. But I also urge us to go slowly. Historical continuity has always been the mark of serious Judaism, and our efforts should respect that as well. The words of prayer keep us rooted in the past, tie us to other Jews of all sorts and in all ages. We should be adding meditation to our worship, creating times and places for Jews to come together in silent awareness of God's presence in our lives. These gatherings will be terribly important for including a new sort of Jew in our community, one who sees himself or herself as a spiritual seeker but feels excluded by the words in which we pray. At the same time, we must keep a place for both the words and the music of traditional prayer to help open our hearts, as they have opened the hearts of Jews for so many generations.

THE 'AMIDAH: STANDING IN GOD'S PRESENCE

The central prayer of Jewish liturgy is called 'amidah, or "the standing." It is to be recited while standing still, focusing attention fully and feeling oneself to be directly in God's presence. The 'amidah was originally to be recited twice daily, at dawn and dusk, in the sacred hour when the light changes from day to night or night to day. These were the times when the daily offering was presented on the Temple altar, and prayer on the heart's altar comes in their place. The Rabbis later added a third daily 'amidah, considered optional by some, to be recited at night.

The 'amidah recited on weekdays contains eighteen blessings; in common Hebrew or Yiddish speech it is thus called shmoneh 'esrey, or "eighteen."[5] Each individual blessing, a few lines to a paragraph in length, concludes with the formula: "Blessed be You, Y-H-W-H..." Of the eighteen blessings, three introduce the 'amidah and three conclude it; these blessings are always present. The twelve intermediate blessings take the form of petitions, asking God to grant wisdom, to forgive sin, to heal, to rebuild Jerusalem, to send messiah, and so forth. On sabbaths and festivals the petitions are eliminated and replaced by a single blessing proclaiming the sanctity of the day.

Many kabbalists over the centuries have composed commentaries to the prayerbook. The meaning of prayer is a subject of

great interest to the mystical tradition, one that wants to reinter-
pret both the *act* and the *text* of prayer in accordance with its own
ways of thinking. What follows is my own brief distillation of
the kabbalistic commentaries on the *'amidah*, in the spirit of understanding the *sefirot* offered above. I share it in the hope of
deepening your experience of prayer and stimulating you to create your own *kavvanot*, or deeper meanings, as you pray.

We begin the *'amidah* by quoting the psalmist, "Lord, open
my lips that my mouth might declare Your praise" (Ps. 51:17).
This is our way of saying that we know from the outset that we
do not pray alone, that God is the *giver* as well as the receiver of
true prayer. This introductory line constitutes a meditation all its
own. Do not rush by it too quickly.

The first blessing, "Shield of Abraham (today many add: 'and
Help of Sarah')," takes us to *ḥesed*, the quality associated with our
first patriarch. Abraham was the true man of *ḥesed* (cf. Micah
7:20); all he did was the result of his endless and unbounded love.
As we recite this blessing, one that describes God in Moses' words
as "great, mighty, and awesome" (Deut. 10:17), we think of the
three qualities of *ḥesed, din,* and *tif'eret;* or love, judgment, and har-
monious balance. Our task is to bundle these three qualities together, in ourselves as in the universe, and to draw them toward
the right, leaning toward the side of *ḥesed*. Although love is not
all there is (in the universe or in ourselves!), we seek to make it
predominate, to subjugate the other *sefirot* to its healing power.
The journey toward full personhood, like our own conception
and journey into life, begins with an act of love. The opening
blessing in the drama of the *'amidah* is also an act of love.

We turn next to the left side in a powerful evocation of life in
the face of death. We confront and accept our mortality, assert-
ing nevertheless that life goes forward and that one can find renewed life even in moments in which death (either physical or
spiritual) seems to triumph. This second blessing, that of *din* or
gevurah, is a confrontation with divine power. It represents Isaac,

the part of our psyche that is tied to the altar, knowing that we are bound to die. It is also the Isaac who, on that very altar, caught a glimpse of eternity, one that he was to carry with him to the end of his long life. We affirm strongly (and in the present tense) that God in each moment of existence sustains the fallen, heals the sick, frees the bound, and resurrects the dead. Thus, we make our peace with the left side, acknowledging the reality of *din* as mortality, judgment, and the limitation of love. In this acceptance we transform its power, accepting *gevurah* with love.

The third blessing, that of Jacob, or *tif'eret*, is stated just briefly when we pray in private. It is the shortest of all of the *'amidah*'s blessings, as though to say that the perfect harmony of "Holy are You!" can last but a moment. The wholeness of Jacob as "the perfect man" (Gen. 25:27) is indeed fleeting; we humans seem to tend toward imbalance. When we have the support of a community praying together, however, this blessing opens to its full glory and becomes the very center of the *'amidah*, the place toward which all of the angels turn in singing "Holy, holy holy!"[6] It is only when we stand together in this place of inner balance and harmony that we can see and proclaim *kedushah*, the holiness and glory of God. Community gives strength and lasting power to our ability to stand in holiness.

The first three blessings of the *'amidah* thus represent the central triad of the *sefirot*, the primal elements out of which our personality is formed. The three blessings that conclude every *'amidah* stand for the lower triad, the second resolution of tensions within the *sefirot*. First of these is *netzah*, the triumphant sense that we can do the task, perfecting both world and self. We ask God to restore the Temple, to bring *shekhinah* back to Zion in all her glory. We will be satisfied with nothing less than true perfection of the world. We seek to bring messiah, the fulfillment of all the ancient prophecies.

As soon as we have said this, however, we realize that we have gone too far. We bow low at *modim*, "we gratefully acknowledge."

We recall how much is done for us by the small and great miracles that happen every day. Our sense of wonder and gratitude is sated by the blessings of ordinary life. We may not be able to perfect the world; we may be fated to live for countless generations in a world without messiah. We learn again to love life as it is, and to accept that which is given. "Your name is good," we conclude, "and it is pleasant to give You thanks."

This second balance leads us to the place of receiving God's greatest blessing, that of peace. At the conclusion of the *'amidah* (parallel to *yesod* or *tzaddik* in the *sefirot)*, is the blessing that the ancient priests pronounced in the Temple: "...May God cause His face to shine upon you and give you peace." In our prayerbook it is paraphrased as "Grant peace," enumerating the many gifts that come to us in the presence of God's shining countenance. We conclude it with a prayer to God "who blesses His people Israel with peace," a blessing much needed in the hour these words are being written.

The last of the seven qualities among the *sefirot* is *malkhut*, or *shekhinah*, the indwelling presence of God. This aspect of divinity is represented by the middle section of the *'amidah*. On weekdays, this takes the form of twelve petitions. *Shekhinah* is the *needy* place, within us and in the cosmos as a whole. We ask for divine help, guidance, healing, and blessing. *We* ask and *shekhinah* asks; there is no clear line of demarcation between these two. It is the call from "below," asking for grace from the mysterious beyond. On Shabbat this same intermediate blessing is one that proclaims fulfillment rather than need. We bless the One who is *mekaddesh ha-shabbat*, who sanctifies the sabbath, but who also weds *shekhinah*.[7] The Divine Presence felt on Shabbat is symbolized by the moment of marriage, the coming together of inner and cosmic "male" and "female" as we realize ourselves as both givers and receivers.

Seen this way, the *'amidah* is an addressing of our own inner selves as we stand in the presence of God's own Self, in whose

2nd Blessing
Gevurot
Gevurah/Isaac
Confronting Mortality
Cycle of Nature: Birth, Death, Rebirth
Affirming Life in the Face of Death
God as Healer, Uplifter

1st Blessing
Avot
Hesed/Abraham
Turn toward God's Love
Faith of Our Ancestors
Joining All to Love
Bow toward Right Side

3rd Blessing
Kedushah
Tif'eret/Jacob
Wholeness, Inner Balance
Fullness of God's Glory
Joining in the Angelic Chorus:
Holy, Holy, Holy!

Weekday
4th–15th Blessings
Bakashot/Petitions
Shekhinah Longs for God's Presence
Pray for the Needs of *Shekhinah* and Soul

Shabbat
4th Blessing
Kedushat ha-Yom
The Holy Day
Shekhinah and Soul Fulfilled
Living in the Light of God's Presence

Shekhinah
King David
Rachel

6th Blessing
Hodayah
Hod/Aaron
Gratitude, Submission
Accepting Life as It Is
Daily Miracles

5th Blessing
Avodah
Netzah/Moses
Striving to Perfect the World
Tikkun 'Olam
Rebuilding the Temple
Bringing Messiah

7th Blessing
Shalom
Yesod/Joseph
Peace, the Vessel to Contain All Blessings
Priestly Blessing
Overflow of Blessing into World
and Soul of the One Who Prays

The Kabbalistic *'Amidah*

image we are made. Each blessing allows for *tikkun*, "repair" or healing of an aspect of personality. Because each personality is unique, and only the individual truly knows where healing is needed, the Rabbis wisely appended to each 'amidah a time for truly silent and private prayer. Here the heart goes back to speaking its own language, offering those gifts that no prayer-book can prescribe.

12

Community: Where *Shekhinah* Dwells

INDIVIDUAL AND COMMUNITY

U NDERSTANDING JUDAISM, and especially the Jewish mystical tradition, as a language of inner quest is the central theme of this book. It is undeniable that there is a lone quality to that journey, one that each person must undertake in his/her own way. The qualities of courage in faith and perseverance required by such a life are essentially those of the individual. Responsibility for establishing the rules and maintaining the seriousness of this quest also belongs ultimately to the seeker alone. Spiritual counsel of a general sort is thus only of limited usefulness. We are reminded of this by a series of Hasidic statements conveying the message that each person must find his/her own path and that imitating others is precisely what *not* to do in the spiritual life.

The lone core of the quest does not mean that we are to pursue it in isolation. Judaism, including Kabbalah, has always been a path that leads to the creation of community, ideally a setting for shared exploration and mutual strengthening by fellow seekers along the way. Outer forms and styles of worship may be very much shared in these communities, giving the superficial observer an image of strict conformity among their members. However, those who dwell at the heart of any religious community know that each person is an entire world and that the struggles and joys that each finds along the path, while shared with others, belong essentially to that soul and to God.

I have lived my own religious life, over these forty and more years, deeply aware of the complex interplay between individual quest and communal concern. As one who lacks the discipline to maintain the very religious life for which I yearn, I long to build community with others who might share such a path. I also know that communal rules themselves can easily become oppressive, causing people like me to flee back to the faulty "freedom" of lone quest. I also care deeply about the Jewish people as a whole, the broader community to which I belong. We are fellow bearers of language, tradition, and history. We are, as the Rabbis proclaimed long ago, "responsible for one another" in a multiplicity of ways. The common fate of Jews as an oppressed and often hated minority through our long history is also a part of my own legacy as a Jew. Over the course of my lifetime, I have several times sought out Jews with whom to create communities of prayer, study, and action with which to change the world.

THE HOLY COMMUNITY

Spring, 1968. Havurat Shalom, a small-scale Jewish community that I had a role in founding, was just in the early stages of moving from dream to reality. We had had a few meetings at the old soon-to-be-abandoned Columbia Street shul in Cambridge, Massachusetts. Several of the remarkable people who were to form that original group had begun to make their appearance. We did not yet have a name for this emerging project. The word "*havurah*" was not yet current in the American Jewish vocabulary, and we did not know in what category to think about the community and alternative seminary of our dreams. I remember that my wife and I drove from

Boston to New York at some point, stopping in New Haven to visit
with our friends Rabbi Richard Israel, of blessed memory, and his
wife, Sherry. Dick, then Hillel director at Yale, was a man who suffered little nonsense. "What are you planning to call this thing?" he
asked. I remember telling him that we were thinking of calling it
Kehillat Kodesh ("Holy Community"). "That's the most pretentious
thing I've ever heard," he said. And so we became Havurat Shalom.

Nonetheless, "Holy Community" is still in my mind, all these
years later. I continue to dream about a group that could live in
the footsteps of Rabbi Simeon ben Yoḥai and the "companions"
of the *Zohar*, or Rabbi Nahman and his disciples in the fields and
woods around Bratslav. The group that Rabbi Nahman wanted is
a little too ascetic for my taste:

> In that place which he had chosen there ran a stream, and be-
> side the stream were fruit trees, and they would eat of the fruit.
> As for clothing—that did not concern them at all; you wore
> whatever you wanted.... There they spent all their time in
> hymns and praises, confessions and fasts, penitence and self-
> mortification. The Master of Prayer would give them some of
> his books, which were filled with hymns and confessions, and
> they would pore over them.[1]

Even so, the dream of a Jewish community fully dedicated to
a life of holiness is one I will carry with me for the rest of my days,
even though I suspect that I would not be capable of living there
for very long.

The original community of that dream is, of course, not
Havurat Shalom, Bratslav, or even the circle of the *Zohar*. It is the
original Jewish community, the one encamped around Mount
Sinai. All of us Jews, whenever in history we were born or chose
to become Jews, were there at Sinai. Occasionally, we like to think,
we remember people from there. A special soul-link happening
between two Jews is most easily explained this way: "Obviously,
we must have been standing next to each other at Mount Sinai."

Actually, two communities were at Sinai. One was at the base of the mountain, a very large group of Jews (a million two hundred thousand, if we accept the biblical number and double it to include the women!) all joined together. They stopped fighting, stopped calling each other names. They had no divisions, no political parties or denominations. There were no Jewish organizations represented at Sinai, only Jews. Nobody worried about whether the Orthodox could stand together with the others Jews, or whether the Reconstructionists had or had not been mentioned. Nobody minded women standing together with the men, and nobody questioned whether the Russians or the Ethiopians were really Jews at all. We stood at the base of the mountain, so we are told, "like a single person, with a single heart."

And that takes us to the other community. Moses ascended the mountain, encountering God at its peak. The later Rabbis say that he even stepped off the mountain and walked into the heavens, holding onto God's throne of glory for protection against the fiery displeasure of the angels, who did not countenance one of flesh and blood walking around in heaven.[2] But Moses did so not just as an individual. He was a *neshamah kelalit,* an all-encompassing "oversoul," one whose soul embraced and held within it all the souls of Israel. Like Adam/Eve at the beginning and messiah at the end, Moses had a soul that included everyone. We therefore were not only at the base of the mountain, but at its top. We were there in the soul of Moses as he entered the heavens. Yes, we are descendents of the poor benighted fools who made the Golden Calf; perhaps that is why we still run so readily after idols. We also bear within us the memory of the most exalted vision. We were there in the soul of the master of all prophets.

Sinai is not just a one-time event. The moment of revelation is forever. Its very nature is the entry of eternity into the flow of time, transforming it—and us—forever.

Every day a voice goes forth from Mount Horeb [Sinai] saying: "Return, O backsliding children!" When will the redemption come? Why, today, of course. "Today if you will listen to His voice" (Ps. 95:7).³ The voice goes forth every day. Sinai is the day when we *listen*.

TWO HALVES OF THE CIRCLE

The community, then, has two faces. It is a community of souls, all of them joined together in a single soul. That is the ultimately mystical side of community. We are all one, a single soul, undivided. Community is also that vast assemblage at the base of the mountain. Here there are bodies, there are different personalities. There must have been screaming children, scared by the lightening. Some of them must have cried so loudly that those around them had trouble hearing. There must have been neighbors with disputes, those same people who had come before Moses in such long, wearying lines, seeking to resolve their differences. At the moment of revelation all of that ceased. Nobody minded anything. We all accepted one another, with all our differences. Gay Jews, straight Jews, Sephardim and Ashkenazim, even *Republican* Jews were welcome at Sinai! The differences remained, but nobody minded.

Religious community requires both of those dimensions. We live with a secret awareness that we are all one. At moments, a glimpse into that reality slips through, sometimes to just one of us, sometimes to a whole group. Community must allow us legitimate ways to share such precious moments, but we must live with others as the community at the base of the mountain. We are real human beings, body as well as soul. We are subject to such real human drives as jealousy, competition, anxiety, and desire. We have fragile egos and bear within us lots of hurt. Something in us is just waiting for an excuse to cry out in pain and resentment. It is with *these* kinds of people that we must live in community.

Loving our fellow Jews is not easy. We are a tough bunch. It is, however, very good training for the bigger task of loving all

of humanity. Remember that one of the Rabbis' rules of interpretation of Scripture reads as follows: "Anything that was part
of a general category and became exceptional did so not only to
teach you about itself, but to teach something regarding the category as a whole."[4] Our fellow Jews are part of the great category called humanity. Loving them, and forming community
with them, is the exception that comes to teach us how to form
human community in general, how to love our fellow person. It
is never just about Jews, but about a paradigm for human relations. If one can make community with a bunch of fractious,
contentious people like "our holy brethren, the whole house of
Israel," loving the rest of humanity should be, as they say, a piece
of cake.

These two aspects of community, mystical oneness and this-
worldly diversity, are nicely captured in a comment by the *Sefat
Emet* on the Sanhedrin, the ancient high court of Israel, a group
of seventy-one elders who are one of our models of sacred community. The Sanhedrin, we should recall, begins when Moses
calls forth seventy wise souls to share with him in receiving the
flow of the Holy Spirit (Num. 11:16). It is the first intentional religious community created among Jews. The Talmud records that
sessions of the Sanhedrin were always seated in a semicircle.
"Why were they seated that way?" asks the *Sefat Emet?* "Because
they were facing the *other* Sanhedrin above, another semicircle
called the heavenly academy in which God and the righteous
study Torah."[5]

Our community is no more than half a circle. Whatever as-
pirations for intimacy we have in this world, we recognize also
the limitations imposed upon us by being diverse human beings,
each with his/her own needs and commitments. But we sit in the
presence of another half circle, one that faces us and challenges
us with a higher truth, the knowledge that we are all one. Any
attempt at sacred community lives in the tension between these
two models.

COMMUNITY AND COVENANT

Because our religious community has its roots at Sinai, it is also a covenanted community. We are joined together by the shared memory of standing at the mountain and by our act of choosing. Before the divine voice came forth, unable to wait for the revelation, all Israel called out *na'aseh ve-nishma'*, "We will do, we will listen." With that act we entered into a covenant, one that continues to make demands upon us. It is idle speculation to ask what would have happened were it not for that upsurge of enthusiasm from within the people. Yes, we heard the voice of God speak, but only after we had agreed to listen. We are therefore already committed, no longer "objective" witnesses to the event. It seems entirely possible that without our declared predisposition to listen, there would have been no voice—or no more voice than comes forth every day, from every mountaintop. It is therefore *we* who establish the covenant; the act of choosing that binds us is our own.

The covenant ties us forever to that moment. Here we are, two months out of Egypt, having been given the great gift of freedom by a power that we are just learning to name. Now we together confront the question, Who do we want to be? What kind of people will be fashioned from these liberated slaves? What is the right way to live in the face of this great transformation that has taken place in our lives? How do we respond in gratitude?

We are still faced with those questions. To be a Jew is to think about the right way to live, to be challenged to respond. Our response must change shape and grow in each generation as it is confronted with new and changing circumstances, but it still grows out of that same challenge. When we live badly, especially when we are mean or ungenerous, we are disgraced before our fellow Jews. "A Jew ought to know better" is something we all feel, the memory of covenant reinforced by, and comingled with, the generations of persecution that also haunt our memory.

The ten commandments of Sinai are the original constitution of this republic of the Jews. All the rest of Torah, we are taught, is rooted in them. Both the spiritual forms and the moral imperatives needed to create the religious life have their origins in these few words. There was once a tendency within Judaism to downplay the importance of the ten commandments. When the Christian Church declared that of the "Old Testament" law only these ten remained binding, Jewish polemicists insisted that we followed all 613 commandments of the Torah, not a mere ten. A poetic and exegetical tradition also emerged among Jews that sought to show how no difference existed between these two claims, as all 613 commandments could be traced back to the original ten.

We would do well to renew that tradition. Jewish communities, both large and small, need codes of conduct. We live in a very open and seemingly unbordered world; this is the source of our anxiety as much as our exhilaration. To live in community is to accept limitations, to be willing to draw borders around our conduct. If used rightly, those chosen self-limitations should help to increase, rather than constrict, our sense of freedom. The old Jewish rule books, grown into the vast edifice called Halakhah, no longer work well for many of us who seek a Jewish path. We therefore need communities that are willing to go back to the Source, to stand together at Sinai, to hear the Word, and to draw conclusions. If we bump and jostle one another as we crowd around the mountain, that too should serve as part of our way of learning.

Each generation is back at Sinai in a unique way, as the Hasidic masters understood so well. The changed circumstances of life, all the more so in an age of rapid transformations such as our own, call for new readings of the ancient text, even new ways to understand and articulate the experience of Sinai itself. Our "new" Torah will become part of the inheritance of the next generation, and that generation will struggle with its legacy as we struggle with the gift and burden of all that has come down to us.

MODELS FROM THE PAST

To engage in this work of living and making Torah requires high levels of both knowledge and commitment. While the task is the same as it always has been, the ways we go about it may be different in our day. It may help us to look at several models of Jewish creativity that come to us from prior generations. In the normative world of Jewish practice, it was the Rabbis, the learned leaders of the people, who "made" Torah. The ongoing legal process, the application of old laws to new situations that in turn formed precedents for further laws, was usually left in the hands of the leading authorities in each generation. Ordinary rabbis would pass their questions on to them and await their answers or responsa. Of course, there were situations, especially in premodern times, when the rabbis were in effect followers rather than leaders, accepting the validity of a new practice or custom because the majority of the people were already doing it. The debate and the decision would take place among the leaders.

The realm of *aggadah*, or spiritual/imaginative creativity, was more open and flexible; any preacher or writer was allowed to innovate in the process of teaching Torah. The mystical tradition has always been especially open to innovative, sometimes even wildly radical, new readings of Torah. In Hasidism the rebbe was seen as a living font of Torah. A new Yiddish expression developed that was used only in the Hasidic context: *Zogn Toireh*, "to say Torah." As the rebbe spoke, new Torah was created. The Hasidim certainly understood that each master had his own way of reading the Scriptures and that the message received as well as the vessel that contained it would vary from teacher to teacher. In short, there is room for individual creativity in responding to the tradition, even respect for the idiosyncrasies of each teacher's viewpoint.

A third model comes to us from the realm of Kabbalah, and that is the notion of a creative circle, a group that engages together in the study of Torah and in seeking out new interpretations. The

primary model for this collective effort at reading and understanding Torah is found in the pages of the *Zohar,* where a community of "companions," fellow students who share a love of one
another as well as of the text before them, inspire one another to
produce ever more innovative and profound readings of verse after
verse. No decision is necessary as to which of these is the "right"
understanding; they stand side by side as part of the collective en-
terprise of interpretation that makes for the *Zohar's* greatness.
This model of creative circles has been followed throughout the
history of Kabbalah, from the Spanish mystics in Gerona and
Castile to circles in Safed, Jerusalem, and towns scattered through
Eastern Europe. On the eve of the Holocaust, Hillel Zeitlin, the
great teacher of Kabbalah to modern Polish Jewry, was calling
for the creation of such a group, a new Yavneh that he hoped
would renew the Jewish creative spirit. Reb Zalman's call for a
Pnai Or, a new Jewish religious order, was in the same spirit.

In our day, I believe that this third model may be especially
valuable. The *ḥavurah,* which I took part in creating more than
thirty years ago, should ideally be a community that combines
passionate learning and creativity, one in which new readings of
Torah are developed in an ongoing conversation among friends,
a project that becomes *our* Torah. The *kabbalah* (remember that
it literally means: "receiving") in such communities should be a
receiving from one another as well as from the text, an openness
and creative energy where sparks of light fly back and forth across
the room. Place should also be made for a deeper *kabbalah,* where
all together can be silent enough to receive from the inner sources
that are present in such a gathering. May God give us the strength
to again create such communities!

Afterword: To Keep on Learning—Where Do I Go from Here?

In order to discover within infinite Torah the teachings that will become *our* Torah, we must become a community of learners. *Talmud Torah*, the process of ongoing learning, is the lifeblood of Judaism. The fitting way for this book to conclude is with a guide to study. Like the rest of the book, it will be written from a highly personal point of view. I am sharing with you some of the Jewish mystical sources that have been important to me in my own journey, hoping that they will also be important in your own reading and study list. Of course yours will (and should) differ somewhat from mine, both because of the nature of our spirits and the history of our journeys. But I still hope this list will be of value to you.

FOR THE BEGINNER

I turn first to the beginner. I am assuming for now that you are a relative novice at Jewish learning, but a serious enough reader to have stayed with me through this book. Where should you go next? My hope is to take you a step beyond the many introductions to Judaism and to Kabbalah that have been written in recent years, although some of them are very fine and will be quite helpful to you. This will be a guide to your further Jewish reading in a broad sense, emphasizing the mystical tradition, but not limited to it.

If you have enjoyed the book you are now reading and want more of this approach, try some of my other books. For beginners, *These Are the Words: A Jewish Spiritual Vocabulary*[1] and *Judaism's Ten Best Ideas: A Brief Guide for Seekers*[2] should be especially helpful. Both are available from Jewish Lights. For further exposure to my own understanding of Judaism, realize that the book you have just read is the middle volume of a theological trilogy. Try going back to my *Seek My Face: A Jewish Mystical Theology*[3] or forward to *Radical Judaism*.[4] The connections between them will become obvious to you. A collection of my essays, scholarly as well as personal and theological, appears under the title *The Heart of the Matter* in the Jewish Publication Society's *Scholars of Distinction* series.[5] A volume with selections of my thought and a fine introductory essay by Ariel Evan Mayse appears in the Library of Contemporary Jewish Philosophers series.[6] You can also access a good number of my articles electronically via my website, artgreen26.com.

Now let me take you back a generation to some of my own teachers and mentors. Abraham Joshua Heschel, the leading voice in Jewish theology in the late twentieth century, was a most gifted writer as well as a profound thinker. Go first to his *God in Search of Man*.[7] Its opening section is the best introduction anywhere to understanding what it means to be a religious person and to be on a seeker's path. Heschel's *The Sabbath*[8] is also a great classic. All of his books are valuable reading. For an initial exposure to him, Fritz Rothschild's selections of Heschel's writings, *Between God and Man*, is useful.[9]

My friend and mentor Reb Zalman Schachter-Shalomi created the Jewish Renewal movement, beginning in the 1980s. He was at his best as an oral teacher, so try to get him on video and in various recorded forms. Of course many of his ideas are available now in print as well. Reb Zalman liked to see himself as a guide to Jewish prayer and practice, rather than as an abstract teacher. The truth is that he was both. His many books published in recent years are mostly collections of occasional talks, edited with the help of various assistants. Those cowritten with Netanel Miles-Yepez are among the best.[10]

Next I would send you a generation back beyond Heschel to the two great neo-Hasidic writers of the early twentieth century, Martin Buber and Hillel Zeitlin. Both of these writers sought to create a new sort of Hasidism appropriate to their own age. For that reason, they read the earlier sources selectively and applied them with a greater universalism than was originally intended. I see my own work as continuing in the tradition they established. Buber's works are widely available in English. I am still partial to his collection *Hasidism and Modern Man*,[11] even though some of the pieces now seem a bit overly romanticized. His essays in a little volume simply entitled *Hasidism* are also worth reading.[12] Zeitlin, a contemporary of Buber's who wrote in Hebrew and Yiddish, lived in Warsaw and perished in the Holocaust. His writings were a particular influence on me, and I have translated a selection of his teachings in *Hasidism for a New Era: The Religious Writings of Hillel Zeitlin*,[13] published in the Paulist Press series Classics of Western Spirituality (a very valuable series to which I will refer regularly, henceforth as CWS). There you will also have a chance to read Joel Rosenberg's especially beautiful translations of Zeitlin's prayers.

Next you should turn to Rabbi Abraham Isaac Kook, a profound mystical teacher who sought a modern idiom in which to express his deeply felt religious insights, informed by Kabbalah but standing outside the kabbalistic and Hasidic traditions. Try the volume of selections from his writings in the same CWS series, edited by Ben Zion Bokser, or the books about him either by Benjamin Ish Shalom[15] or Yehudah Mirsky.[15] Kook, like

Zeitlin, is little known among North American Jews, but is very widely read and studied in Israel. Because he is the leading spiritual figure within religious Zionism, mystical ideas have had a great influence on Israeli understandings of Judaism.

LEARNING HEBREW

If you've made your way through this volume, you are starting to get quite serious about your Jewish learning. Here we have to talk about Hebrew. Face it: ultimately Judaism does not work very well in translation. I say this to you despite the fact that I have spent many years translating Hasidic works from Hebrew into English. I even like to think that I am pretty good as a translator. Still, it's not the same. The Jewish mystical tradition was created by people who loved the Hebrew language, who believed in it as the sacred tongue. They believed that Hebrew was the language of God, the vehicle through which the world was created. They therefore saw profound mysteries in the language itself, in its sounds, the shapes of its letters, the inner connections between word roots, the oddities of biblical syntax and spelling, and all the rest. While on the level of rational thought we may not accept their assumptions, we need to be able to join them in this way of close reading in order to enter into their mindset and understand their teachings, which are often truly profound and exciting precisely in the way they unpack linguistic details. To do so through translation, with footnotes added to explain the puns and word-plays, turns a "light" way of reading into something burdensome. Translation is indeed, as they say, like kissing the bride through a veil—a veil of footnotes!

So get to work on your Hebrew. The more you know, the better. I am going to suggest lots of things to study in translation, but that's what to do along the way, *while* you are learning Hebrew, not instead of it. But first, let me say a little more about the Hebrew you will need. I'm not talking about modern conversational Hebrew, although a beginning course in conversation is sometimes a good way to start on the language. You also don't want the typical Christian seminary approach to biblical Hebrew, where you spend too much time memorizing grammatical rules and never quite get a sense of the life that dwells within the language.

Learn Hebrew as a *Jewish* language. Start learning it in the synagogue and through the siddur (prayerbook). Go to a shul (synagogue) with a fairly traditional Hebrew liturgy every week and follow the service carefully. Use your siddur every day, whether for *davnen,* reading psalms, or whatever else works for you as a devotional exercise. Use a translation to help you get the meaning of the Hebrew. Try one of the interlinear translations and see if you find that more helpful. Ask yourself *why* that word or group of words results in that particular meaning in English. Figure it out. Learn to parse words and to find their roots. The root system of Hebrew is a great guide to associative thinking. Eventually you will get to the point where you can leave the English behind for that particular prayer or psalm. Now you can understand what you're saying without a translation. It's a great feeling! (You will have time later to deal with how you feel about the theology of some of those lines; here the siddur is serving as your Hebrew lesson.)

Do the same with Torah. Start reading the weekly Torah portion in Hebrew, as much as you can. The old way of preparing for Shabbat was supposed to include reading the weekly Torah portion "twice in Hebrew, once in [Aramaic] translation." I hereby grant you permission to substitute English for the Aramaic (that is the only halakhic decision you will find in this book). Once you can read and understand simple portions of the Torah narrative, along with the siddur, you're doing *very* well. Congratulations! You are well on your way to becoming a literate Jew. The Torah and the siddur are the most basic texts of the tradition; almost everything else is a commentary on them. Keep working on

Torah; the better you know this text, the better off you'll be in all that comes after it. If you want to enrich your curricular diet with some great stories, I recommend Jonah, Ruth, and the Elijah/ Elisha stories in the first book of Kings (beginning with chapter 17). The Hebrew in these is relatively simple and quite beautiful. You will be amply rewarded by the stories themselves.

Now you are ready to tackle the Hebrew of the Rabbis, and that's what you'll need most to study the mystical and Hasidic sources. You've already encountered some rabbinic forms in the siddur, but now you're on to "the real thing." I'd start with some selections from the Mishnah (*Berakhot*, the opening tractate on prayer, will do quite nicely) and, at the same time, Rashi's commentary on the Torah, which for centuries has been a most basic text of Jewish learning. It also happens to be available in a couple of Hebrew/English versions. Along with these, you might try a little *aggadah*, collections of rabbinic tales and narratives. The classic modern collection is Bialik and Ravnitsky's *Sefer ha-Aggadah*, and here too you will find an English translation to help you along with your Hebrew.[16]

BEGINNING TO STUDY KABBALAH

Unlike the situation just a generation ago, there are now a great many books on Jewish mysticism available for the English reader. These include primary sources in translation, academic studies, and introductions in seekers' guides of various sorts. Especially in this last category, the quality of such works varies greatly, so careful selection is important. We'll begin here in reverse order, starting with the guides, looking briefly at scholarly works, and then turning to the sources themselves.

Two faithful guides speaking from within the mystical tradition are Aryeh Kaplan and Rabbi Adin Steinsaltz. Their various works, while somewhat lacking when it comes to history, are faithful to the intent of the original Kabbalistic sources and are written in a welcoming style. Best-known of these is Steinsaltz's *The Thirteen-Petalled Rose*,[17] probably a good starting place. For another sort of introduction, one lighter on information but rich in contemporary insight, try Lawrence Kushner's *The River of Light*.[18] For an accessible survey of Kabbalah written by an academic scholar, David Ariel's *Kabbalah: The Mystic Quest* will serve well.[19]

Even if your interest is in personal and spiritual edification, there is nothing wrong with reading some of the great historians of Jewish mysticism to gain more basic information. Don't expect them to be your spiritual guides, but use their writings as ways to prepare yourself for the study of texts. Gershom Scholem is the great academic master of this field, even decades after many questions have been raised about some of his theories. His book *Kabbalah*,[20] a collection of his essays for the *Encyclopedia Judaica*, is somewhat dry but packed with information. The same is true of his *Major Trends in Jewish Mysticism*,[21] the standard historical survey. That work is now considered dated, but is still essential reading. "Juicier" readings by Scholem are his collected essays in *On the Kabbalah and Its Symbolism*[22] and *On the Mystical Shape of the Godhead*.[23] Joseph Dan's multivolume historical survey *Jewish Mysticism*[24] is in the Scholem tradition and is written in an accessible style. For more daring and innovative approaches to Kabbalah scholarship today, look at the writings of Moshe Idel (*Kabbalah: New Perspectives*[25] and *Absorbing Perfections*[26] are his best English works), Yehuda Liebes (see his two little volumes of collected English *Studies*, published by SUNY Press;[27] the rest is only in Hebrew), and Elliot Wolfson (*Through a Speculum That Shines*[28] is the place to start). Idel and Wolfson are both wonderfully filled with knowledge and insight, though neither is easy to read. Be prepared to work hard when tackling them. Other scholars of Kabbalah whose works are available in English include Lawrence Fine, Jonathan Garb, Joel Hecker, and Eitan Fishbane.

That's enough of scholarship, which is not the main point here. It is time to get to the sources. I suggest that the early kabbalistic books, especially the *Zohar*, and the Hasidic masters are the right combination to provide a basis for a contemporary Kabbalah. I am not a great fan of the later kabbalistic tradition, that which tried to follow in the footsteps of Rabbi Isaac Luria, a truly great kabbalist of the sixteenth century. I find that the post-Lurianic works tend to get overly convoluted, afflicted by the same spirit of hair-splitting *pilpul* (that's "casuistry" in English) that mostly ruined Jewish legal thought in the same period. I also find the earlier model of the ten *sefirot* to be more useful than the Lurianic reconfiguration into five "countenances" and six stages of spiritual maturation. I will therefore not be recommending works of the Lurianic tradition, even though I know that will put me at odds with the contemporary Jerusalem kabbalists, who study the old traditions *only* through the Lurianic prism. I consider that a great mistake.[29] When you are a truly advanced student of Kabbalah, try the Lurianic methods as well, but not now.

My student Ariel Evan Mayse has edited a fine historically based anthology of Jewish mystical texts entitled *From the Depth of the Well*, using the many works translated in the CWS series.[30] That will give you an opportunity to "taste and see" sources from nearly every age and genre. Study them slowly and use them as points of departure for your own meditations. Doing so will also offer you an indication of which texts most appeal to your own spirit, allowing you to make choices about where to go deeper. There is room for a great array of diverse spiritual personality types within the vast literature of Jewish mysticism. Some soaring spirits are attracted to Merkavah accounts of journeys through the upper realms. Others, much more earthbound in their spiritual goals, will be more comfortable amid the teachings of Polish Hasidic masters of the nineteenth century. Some will be "drawn into the chambers of the King" through the poetry of the *Zohar*'s dazzling sefirotic symbolism. There are those, unlike myself, who find fulfillment in the infinitely complex pathways of the Lurianic system of intentions for the religious life and permutations of the divine name. All of these are legitimate ways of seeking spiritual nourishment within the Jewish mystical tradition. Alongside *From the Depth of the Well*, I recommend your reading Louis Jacobs's *Jewish Mystical Testimonies*.[31] There Jacobs has brought together actual accounts of religious experience, culled from a great variety of sources.

Studying the *Zohar* is a great treat for any student of Kabbalah. Once you start reading *Zohar* you'll never stop, so be prepared for a lifelong engagement. By far our best *Zohar* teacher for the English-language reader is Daniel Matt. Begin with his little anthology *Zohar: The Book of Enlightenment*,[32] being sure to read the notes in the back of the book along with the passages. In these brief selections, Matt gives you a wonderful taste of what is in store for you as you delve into the *Zohar* itself.[33] You now can do so through the magnificent twelve-volume Pritzker edition of the *Zohar*, published by Stanford University Press.[34] The first nine volumes of the set are translated and commented upon by Matt, the three others also by very fine *Zohar* scholars. I believe it no exaggeration to say that this edition renders the *Zohar* readable for the first time in any language. None of the many Hebrew commentaries written over the centuries explicates the *Zohar* as fully as Matt and his colleagues do.

A page of the *Zohar* should be read slowly and contemplatively. Open your mind as the *Zohar* has "opened" the Torah text for you. See the Torah through the prism of *sefirot* as the *Zohar* has done, but also go beyond "plugging in" to the symbols to see the grand sweep of the *Zohar*'s vision. Enter into the rich stories of the *Zohar*'s heroes, and watch how the accounts of their adventures and encounters in this world interplay with what is happening in the worlds beyond. As you begin reading the *Zohar*, you might want to look at my own introduction, either in brief form in the first volume of the Pritzker edition, or more fully in the separate volume *A Guide to the Zohar*, also published by Stanford. For a fuller exposition of themes and ideas within the *Zohar*, see

Wisdom of the Zohar by Isaiah Tishby,[35] one of Scholem's disciples, which in three volumes will give you very detailed accounts of subjects covered in that work, illustrated by translated passages. Look especially at the early sections on *sefirot* and *shekhinah*, but also at some of the materials on the commandments: Shabbat, holidays, and so forth. The English translation of Tishby unfortunately offers somewhat dry and prosaic renditions of the beautifully poetic *Zohar* text. Always compare these to Matt's translations, which are much better at conveying the poetic and ambiguously symbolic tones. Tishby is best used as a reference work when you want to research a subject, rather than as a text to read for inspiration. Another important and beautifully poetic reading of the *Zohar* is found in Melila Hellner-Eshed's *A River Flows from Eden*.[36]

A classical guide to the language of Kabbalah as well as its spirit is R. Joseph Gikatilia's *Sha'arey Orah*. Gikatilia was a contemporary of the *Zohar*, a close member of the circle from which it emerged. There is a good English translation, *Gates of Light*, but if you know some Hebrew, use the English and Hebrew together.[37] The book is a stroll through the ten *sefirot*, offering a deep immersion into kabbalistic symbolism. It is great preparation for the study of the *Zohar*, but can also be read alongside it.

Among the other kabbalistic books available in English, you would do well to choose the selections in *Safed Spirituality*[38] and the portion of Isaiah Horowitz's monumental *Two Tablets of the Covenant*, translated by Miles Krassen.[39] Horowitz's book, written in seventeenth-century Jerusalem, was widely studied in Eastern Europe and was an important influence on the shaping of Hasidism. A special treatise on Shabbat through the eyes of the kabbalist is *Sod ha-Shabbat*, a portion of R. Meir Ibn Gabbai's commentary on the prayerbook. It has been translated by Elliot Ginsburg, along with a companion volume called *The Sabbath in the Classical Kabbalah*.[40] You can learn a great deal about Kabbalah and its symbolism from a careful reading of Ginsburg's very rich and interesting notes. For a rare and very important introduction to Kabbalah as an ethical system, see R. Moses Cordovero's *The Palm Tree of Deborah*, translated by Louis Jacobs.[41]

Much of Kabbalah appears in the form of Biblical commentary. A favorite of the *Zohar* and the entire kabbalistic tradition is the Song of Songs, the great love poem between God and the seeking soul. Michael Fishbane has just published a marvelous fourfold commentary to the Song. The *remez* and *sod* levels within it essentially constitute a very beautiful philosophical and kabbalistic commentary, the first one ever composed in English. I highly recommend it, as both an intellectual and devotional treat.[42]

FOR THE HEBREW READER

Now I turn back to the Hebrew reader. I have in mind one who has chosen to read this book in English (a Hebrew edition is currently in the works), but has the ability to read classical Hebrew sources. The same path is a good one for you. After spending some time with *Sha'arey Orah*, begin studying *Zohar*. There are a couple of adequate Hebrew translations of the entire *Zohar*. In some of these you will find the Aramaic text vocalized, an additional help in reading. (I suggest you avoid the *Sulam* and the other works by Rabbi Ashlag and his school at this stage, as they intersperse the translation with commentaries in the Lurianic framework, and that is simply confusing.) A worthwhile contemporary commentary, along with Hebrew translation, is found in a work called *Yedid Nefesh*, but there too you will have to resist the Lurianic readings. Go back and forth between the Aramaic and the Hebrew until you find the Hebrew no longer necessary. Still, as you read the Aramaic, translate mentally into Hebrew; that will often be a help in understanding, since the authors themselves were essentially doing the reverse.

My favorite partly kabbalistic Torah commentary is that of R. Baḥya ben Asher, *Rabbenu Baḥya 'al ha-Torah*, available in a very attractive Mossad ha-Rav Kook edition. R. Baḥya follows the fourfold model of interpreting Torah: "plain" meaning, midrash, philosophical readings, and Kabbalah. His Hebrew is quite readable and his interpretations are often exciting. Parallel to him is R. Menahem Recanati, whose classical kabbalistic reading of the Torah is interspersed with quotations from the *Zohar.* For a commentary on the prayerbook, use R. Meir Ibn Gabbai's *Tola'at Ya'akov.* If you are ready for a grand introduction to Kabbalah as a system, the first two sections of Ibn Gabbai's *'Avodat ha-Kodesh* are a wonderful treasure, written in clear and lovely Hebrew prose, and now available in a readable, modern print edition.[43] Ibn Gabbai directly influenced Horowitz's *Shney Luḥot ha-Berit,*[44] a great compendium of Jewish mystical piety.

HASIDISM AND ITS TEACHINGS

Now we are ready to turn to Hasidism, first for the English reader. There are several good anthologies and introductions that will help you enter the world of Hasidic teachings. My own contribution, edited with several of my closest students, is *Speaking Torah: Spiritual Teachings from around the Maggid's Table.*[45] There we offer selections from over forty early Hasidic classics, following the weekly portion and holiday cycle. Each teaching, printed in both Hebrew and English, is followed by a brief comment. At the end of each weekly portion, we record a "round two" of our own conversation around the texts. We intend it especially for readers such as you, providing an entryway to the study of Hasidic sources. If you are looking for an anthology arranged by subject matter rather than Torah portion, *The Religious Thought of Hasidism* by Norman Lamm[46] is quite useful.

Speaking Torah opens with a long introduction to early Hasidism, with an emphasis on aspects of Hasidic thought. I have a number of others essays on this subject, available either in *The Heart of the Matter* or on my website. For other scholarly approaches to Hasidic thought, Joseph Dan's *The Teachings of Hasidism*[47] is a usable introduction. Rivka Schatz-Uffenheimer's *Hasidism as Mysticism: Quietistic Elements in Eighteenth-Century Hasidic Thought*[48] and Rachel Elior's *The Paradoxical Ascent to God: The Kabbalistic Theosophy of Habad Hasidism*[49] are among the academic classics, although Schatz-Uffenheimer's conclusions are now much debated by more recent scholarship in Hebrew. For Polish Hasidism of the nineteenth century, see Michael Rosen's *The Quest for Authenticy: The Thought of Reb Simhah Bunim*.[50] The new *History of Hasidism*, edited by David Biale and a committee of scholars, sees its main focus as social history.[51] But it too will contain some valuable insights.

Now to the Hasidic sources themselves, once you want to go beyond anthologies and secondary works. You can do no better than to start with the second section of the *Tanya* by R. Shneur Zalman of Liadi, the founder of what was to become ḤaBaD, or Lubavitch Hasidism. This text, also called "The Treatise on Unity and Faith," is translated by the Chabad Hasidim and is available through their Kehot Publishing Company. It is a concise and well-argued introduction to mystical consciousness in a Jewish context.

I have translated portions of two of my favorites of Hasidic teachings, and you might next want to study those texts. One is the *Me'or 'Eynayim* by R. Menahem Nahum of Chernobyl. The published edition[52] covers only the Book of Genesis, but I soon hope to offer a translation of the entire work. R. Nahum, as he is called, was one of the most important early Hasidic masters. His book stays extremely close to what I believe was the original message of the Ba'al Shem Tov (himself an oral teacher who did not write books), and for that reason it is especially significant. The other is the *Sefat Emet* by R. Yehudah Leib Alter of Ger. My collection of bilingual selections, with a commentary of my own, is called *The Language of Truth*.[53] The *Sefat Emet* represents a later example of Hasidic writings by a Polish master who lived into the

beginning of the twentieth century. The original work is volumi-
nous; I offer only a very small portion of it. The Hebrew reader
will hopefully find many years' pleasure and challenge in it, as
I have.

Instructions for prayer and the devotional life constitute an
important part of Hasidic teaching as well, often presented in
concise and accessible form. The *Upright Practices* I translated
together with the *Me'or 'Eynayim* are a good example of this. The
many oral prayer instructions offered by the Ba'al Shem Tov
were recorded by disciples over the years. I (together with Barry
Holtz) translated a brief selection of these as *Your Word Is Fire*
many years ago.[54] Now the entire collection has been translated,
with extensive commentary, by Menachem Kallus as *The Pillar
of Prayer*.[55]

Among later Hasidic masters, the *Mey ha-Shiloaḥ* by R. Mordecai
Joseph of Izbica is a particularly rich and sometimes quite daring work. Izbica represents a unique sub-school within Polish
Hasidism, and there is a great revival of interest in it in recent
years, especially in Israel. Morris Faierstein[56] and Shaul Maggid[57]
have both written on Izbica and its teachings. Several works by
Rabbi Kalonymos Kalmish Shapira of Piasecne, an innovative
twentieth-century Hasidic master and martyr of the Warsaw
ghetto, have also been translated. See the study of him by
Nehemia Polen.[58]

Hasidic tales are a genre of originally oral literature that were
later written down and passed across the generations. The first
collection was *Shivhey ha-BeSHT,* published in 1815. It is translated
by Dan Ben-Amos and Jerome Mintz as *In Praise of the Ba'al Shem
Tov*.[59] There are hundreds of little volumes of these tales available in Hebrew and Yiddish. Of the many English anthologies,
I am still partial to Martin Buber's *Tales of the Hasidim* (despite
his tendency to reshape some tales for his Western audience)
and Jiří Langer's *Nine Gates to the Chasidic Mysteries*.[60] Zalman
Schachter-Shalomi also has edited several collections of tales,

including *Wrapped in a Holy Flame: Teachings and Tales of the Hasidic Masters.*[61]

A special category of Hasidic writings is the teachings and tales of R. Nahman of Bratslav (Breslov), a unique and enigmatic figure of Jewish spiritual history. His teachings have been translated, with commentary, in many volumes published by the Breslov Research Institute. The reader should be warned, however, that R. Nahman is difficult to read, perhaps especially in translation. Even more than others, he uses a sort of associative thinking that depends entirely on links between terms and concepts that will be lost in translation. His teachings are therefore not recommended for beginners. The much more accessible if enigmatic *Tales* have been translated into English several times. My own favorite English version is that of Arnold Band,[62] but the commentary by Aryeh Kaplan is also quite worth reading.[63] If you want to learn something about R. Nahman and his teachings, my biography of him, *Tormented Master*,[64] is available from Jewish Lights.

HASIDISM FOR THE HEBREW READER

The Hebrew reader can choose from a great wealth of Hasidic sources, including all those already mentioned. Some other favorites that I have taught and studied over the years are the *Degel Maḥaneh Ephraim* by the Ba'al Shem Tov's grandson R. Ephraim of Sudilkow and *Kedushat Levi* by R. Levi Yizhak of Berdichev, one of the best known and most beloved of the Hasidic masters. Many of these works have been reprinted in recent Israeli editions that are more "user-friendly" than the old ones, providing punctuation, lists of sources, and occasionally even vocalization. The same is true of the *Sefat Emet* and Breslov writings. Many readers today enjoy studying the *Netivot Shalom*, written by the Slonimer rebbe of Jerusalem who passed away only a few years ago. He writes in an intriguing mixture of Hasidic and modern Hebrew.

INTERNET RESOURCES

I should also mention some of the many electronic resources for Jewish learning that are now available to us. These grant unparalleled access to an enormous number of our religious texts, without requiring an inquisitive seeker to immediately purchase an extensive (and expensive!) collection of books. However, a brief note of caution is also in order: as it is with anything on the Internet, the online world of Jewish learning has some unfortunate pockets of misinformation. This certainly shouldn't stop you from making use of the great number of authentic computerized resources, but do remember to have this caveat in mind whenever you read electronic materials (especially if they're not primary sources).

The English reader might be encouraged to explore the library section of www.chabad.org. This website offers useful and accessible translations of several dozen of the primary works of ḤaBaD mystical thought, which will doubtless hold inspiration for the beginner and more experienced learner alike. In addition, the English versions of these texts often contain excellent bibliographical footnotes that can help guide the reader back to the earlier Jewish sources upon which the later Hasidic works are built. Readers with more confidence in their Hebrew may find computer programs like the Bar-Ilan Responsa Project or Otzar HaHochma to be fantastic assets. These electronic databases each contain thousands of classical Jewish works and allow us to either browse among or to search through the books instantly by keyword or phrase. Similarly, the website www.hebrewbooks. org offers free access to tens of thousands of Jewish books, and even this surprising number is constantly increasing. All of these texts, many of which are rare and out of print, can be immediately downloaded at no cost. Even better, unlike the books contained in computerized databases (which have been totally reformatted to fit their new medium), the works available at www.hebrewbooks.org have been simply scanned directly from the original—the electronic version of the page is exactly the same as that of the book from which it was taken. For those of us who grew up reading from pages rather than screens, this website provides a much more comfortable middle ground, and its informational and bibliographical value cannot be overestimated. In sum, although you may find that they don't fully substitute for the experience of sitting in front of a physical book and learning, computer programs and Internet sites can be an important resource along your journey into Jewish learning.

Studying the Hasidic and kabbalistic sources has been a great source of spiritual nourishment for me over the course of these fifty years. I would be delighted to learn that this book, or perhaps some other writing of mine, helped bring you to those sources and that you, too, have deepened your quest through reading and studying them, especially in the Hebrew. At the same time, I am well aware that you and I are not part of the traditional Hasidic community. That is the result of a conscious decision on my part, and probably on yours as well. For people such as ourselves, the teachings of prior generations are not the end of the journey. We study them to deepen our own roots in the tradition and to be inspired by the profundity of their teachings, but ultimately they stand as a challenge to our own creativity. We need to do for our age what the kabbalistic and Hasidic masters did for theirs. We need to find a way to read the Torah that will open the gates of both the written word and of our own souls. We seek a reading that will bring us, as the very post-modern seekers that we are, face to face with the eternal voice that still calls to us from within the text. In this, the masters of prior ages can be our guides, but they cannot substitute for the work that is ours alone. That task still lies before us. In that context, I would like to conclude by sharing with you a very daring interpretation of the blessing we recite following the reading of a section of the weekly

Torah portion. This teaching is found in several places within the *Sefat Emet*, mentioned above. The blessing reads: "Blessing to You, Y-H-W-H our God, universal Ruler, who has given us the Torah of truth and implanted eternal life within us. Blessing to You, Y-H-W-H, giving Torah." The *Sefat Emet* says that "The Torah of truth" refers to written Torah, while "eternal life within us" denotes the Oral Torah. (Note that "Oral Torah" here is not a body of literature, written in the past, but an ongoing, living process!) Only when the two aspects of Torah come together is the giving of Torah transformed from a past event into one of the eternal present.

Go forth and reveal Torah!

Notes

Confession, by Way of a Preface

1. The true beginner might do well to acquire a copy of my book *These Are the Words: A Vocabulary of Jewish Spiritual Life* (Woodstock, Vt.: Jewish Lights, 2000). There I offer brief definitions of some key terms of the Jewish religious tradition, many of which will be discussed in this book as well.

2. Hillel Zeitlin, *In the Garden of Hasidism and Kabbalah* (Tel Aviv: Yavneh, 1960).

3. I spent many years studying the life and teachings of this famed Hasidic master (1772–1810). You may want to see my book *Tormented Master: The Life and Spiritual Quest of Rabbi Nahman of Bratslav* (Woodstock, Vt.: Jewish Lights, 1992).

4. *Sippurim Nifla'im*, edited by Samuel Horowitz (Jerusalem, 1961), p. 26 (adapted). See *Tormented Master*, p. 181, n. 73, for discussion of this tale.

5. Both essays are included in *The New Jews*, edited by A. Mintz and J. Sleeper (New York: Vintage Books, 1971).

6. The commandments are to serve as reminders of God's redeeming presence. The phrase is from Numbers 15:40, and refers originally to the fringed garment. It is quoted in the *Shema'* of daily prayers.

Introduction: Ehyeh as a Name of God

1. *Bereshit Rabbah* 68:10.

KABBALAH OLD AND NEW

1. A follower of Hasidism is called a Hasid (pl.: Hasidim). The term can be translated either as "devotee" or "disciple."

THERE IS ONLY ONE

1. Adapted from *Keter Shem Tov* (New York: Otsar ha-Hasidim, 1987), f. 8a (#51).
2. I have published a selection of his teachings in English translation, *The Language of Truth: The Torah Commentary of the Sefat Emet, Rabbi Yehudah Leib Alter of Ger* (Philadelphia: Jewish Publication Society, 1998).
3. *Otsar Ma'amarim u-Mikhtavim* (Jerusalem: Makhon Gaḥaley Esh, 1986), p. 75f.
4. See discussion of *keter* in the Introduction.

TORAH: CREATION'S TRUTH REVEALED

1. *Mishnah Avot* 5:1.
2. *Zohar* 3:221a.
3. Moses Maimonides, *The Guide of the Perplexed* 3:51. Translated by Shlomo Pines (Chicago: University of Chicago Press, 1963), p. 623f.
4. See *The Language of Truth*, pp. 3f, 326f, and 403f.
5. See my prior discussion of this point in *Seek My Face: A Jewish Mystical Theology* (Woodstock, Vt.: Jewish Lights, 2003), p. 95f.
6. *Rosh Hashanah* 32a.
7. *Seder Eliyahu Zuta* 2.

SEFIROT: THE ONE AND THE TEN

1. I have traced the history of this influence in *Keter: The Crown of God in Early Jewish Mysticism* (Princeton: Princeton University Press, 1997).
2. Zevi Hirsch of Zydachow, *'Ateret Zevi, parashat aharey mot* (Jerusalem, 1960), f. 25a.

'OLAMOT: FOUR STEPS TO ONENESS

1. *Yedid Nefesh* was composed by R. Eleazar Azikri of Safed (1533–1600). The original manuscript of this poem, written in his own hand, is in the library of The Jewish Theological Seminary in New York.
2. From *Adon 'Olam*, familiar from the daily prayerbook, author unknown.

SHEMOT: THE WAY OF NAMES

1. *Pesahim* 50a.
2. The reader looking for further reflection on the name may want to go to my book *Seek My Face.* The entire book is structured as a meditation on the name Y-H-W-H.

SEEKING A PATH

1. See *Berakhot* 10a.
2. An English translation of this Hebrew can be found in Louis Jacobs, *Jewish Mystical Testimonies* (New York: Schocken Books, 1977), p. 148f.
3. *Me'or 'Eynayim, Liqqutim* to *Parashat Bereshit* (Jerusalem, 1986), p. 224.
4. As far back as the fifteenth century a tradition of Christian Kabbalah also began to develop, based on translations of Hebrew and Aramaic sources into Latin. Out of this came later Western occultism and theosophical study of Kabbalah, but these became separated quite completely from their Jewish origins.
5. See Rabbi Hayyim Ibn 'Attar, *Or ha-Ḥayyim* to Exodus 39:32.
6. *Berakhot* 5b.

GREAT CHAIN OF BEING: KABBALAH FOR AN ENVIRONMENTAL AGE

1. Arthur Green, *Devotion and Commandment: The Faith of Abraham in the Hasidic Imagination* (Cincinnati: Hebrew Union College Press, 1989).

ALL ABOUT BEING HUMAN: IMAGE, LIKENESS, MEMORY

1. The poems have been translated/adapted into an English version by Zalman M. Schacter-Shalomi in *Human: God's Ineffable Name* (privately printed, n.p., 1973).
2. *Liqqutey MoHaRaN* 1:282.
3. *Pirkei Avot* 5:6.
4. See Rabbi Nahman's *The Tales,* translated by Arnold Band (New York: Paulist Press, 1978), pp. 260–262.

WHAT ABOUT EVIL?

1. *Mekhilta Pisḥa* 14.
2. *Ma'asiyot ve-Siḥot Tsaddikim,* cited by Martin Buber in *Or ha-Ganuz* (Jerusalem: Schocken Books, 1958), p. 226.

3. See Gershom Scholem, *On the Mystical Shape of the Godhead* (New York: Schocken Books, 1991), pp. 65–68.
4. *Ḥullin* 60b.
5. See *Zohar* 3:22a, etc.

THE LIFE OF PRAYER

1. *Your Word Is Fire: The Hasidic Masters on Contemplative Prayer,* edited and translated by Arthur Green and Barry W. Holtz (Woodstock, Vt.: Jewish Lights, 1993).
2. *Midrash Pinḥas* (Jerusalem, n.d. [195–?]), p. 18f.
3. A more literal reading renders it, "As for me, my prayer is to You, O Lord."
4. *Toldot Ya'akov Yosef* 1696b. Cited in *Your Word Is Fire,* p. 70.
5. Traditional prayerbooks now actually include nineteen rather than eighteen blessings in the *'amidah*. The addition is because of a blessing called *birkat ha-minim,* ("the blessing of heretics"), actually a calling down of divine wrath on heretics (these included the earliest Jewish Christians, among others) and "informers," those who collaborated with governments that persecuted Jews. Its meaning was later expanded to be a denunciation of wickedness in general and a call for its destruction. As one who has been called a heretic more than once, I find it unseemly to pray for their downfall. I have deleted this blessing from my own prayers, happily restoring the *'amidah* to a proper eighteen. I invite others to consider joining me in this change.
6. When the morning or afternoon *'amidah* is recited publicly (amid a quorum of ten or more), it is repeated aloud by the prayer leader. In that *'amidah,* the third blessing is lengthened to include the *kedushah,* a series of responses opening with Isaiah 6:3: "They called to one another, saying, "Holy, Holy, Holy is the Lord of Hosts; the whole earth is filled with His glory."
7. The Hebrew *mekaddesh* can be read to mean either "sanctify" or "wed."

COMMUNITY: WHERE *SHEKHINAH* DWELLS

1. From Rabbi Nahman's tale *The Master of Prayer,* cited in *Tormented Master,* p. 152.
2. *Shabbat* 88b.

3. Talmud, *Sanhedrin* 98a.
4. The "thirteen rules of Rabbi Ishmael," taken from the opening of the Sifra, an ancient midrash on Leviticus, are found in the traditional daily morning service.
5. *The Language of Truth*, p. 159f.

AFTERWORD: TO KEEP ON LEARNING—WHERE DO I GO FROM HERE?
1. 2nd Edition (Woodstock, Vt.: Jewish Lights, 2012).
2. Woodstock, Vt.: Jewish Lights, 2014.
3. Woodstock, Vt.: Jewish Lights, 2003.
4. New Haven: Yale University Press, 2010.
5. Philadelphia: Jewish Publication Society, 2015.
6. *Arthur Green: An Intellectual Portrait* (Leiden, Neth.: Brill, forthcoming).
7. New York: Farrar, Straus, and Giroux, 1955.
8. New York: Farrar, Straus, and Giroux, 1951.
9. New York: Free Press, 1959.
10. His more important theoretical works include *Paradigm Shift* (Northvale, N.J.: Jason Aronson, 1993) and *Credo of a Modern Kabbalist* (Victoria, BC: Trafford, 2005).
11. New York: Harper and Row, 1966.
12. New York: Philosophical Library, 1948.
13. Mahwah, N.J.: Paulist Press, 2012.
14. Benjamin Ish Shalom, *Rav Avraham Itzhak HaCohen Kook: Between Rationalism and Mysticism* (Albany: SUNY Press, 1993).
15. *Rav Kook: Mystic in a Time of Revolution* (New Haven: Yale University Press, 2014).
16. *The Book of Legends*, trans. by William G. Braude (New York: Schocken Books, 1992).
17. New York: Basic Books, 1980.
18. Woodstock, Vt.: Jewish Lights, 1990.
19. New York: Schocken Books, 1992.
20. New York: Quadrangle/New York Times Book Co., 1974.
21. With a foreword by Robert Alter (New York: Schocken Books, 1995).
22. Translated by Ralph Manheim (New York: Schocken Books, 1965).
23. New York: Schocken Books, 1991.
24. Northvale, N.J.: Jason Aronson, 1998–1999.

25. New Haven: Yale University Press, 1988.

26. New Haven: Yale University Press, 2002.

27. *Studies in the Zohar* and *Studies in Jewish Myth and Jewish Messianism* (Albany: SUNY Press, 1993).

28. Princeton: Princeton University Press, 1994.

29. For this reason I do not recommend the writings of Rabbi Yehuda Leib Ashlag or his various disciples. Ashlag was indeed a serious and important thinker for whom I have high regard. But the post-Ashlag schools, as their works have proliferated, have gone astray in various ways, either by overpopularization or overly technical Lurianism. I find both of these unhelpful. On the Ashlag schools and their recent history, see Jonathan Garb's *The Chosen Will Become Herds: Studies in Twentieth-Century Kabbalah* (New Haven: Yale University Press, 2009).

30. Mahwah, N.J.: Paulist Press, 2014.

31. Jerusalem: Keter Books, 1976.

32. Mahwah, N.J.: Paulist Press, 1983.

33. Matt has also written a beginners' volume, *Zohar: Annotated & Explained* (Woodstock, Vt.: SkyLight Paths, 2002).

34. *The Zohar: Pritzker Edition*, 12 vols. (Stanford, Calif.: Stanford University Press, 2003–).

35. Translated by David Goldstein (London: Littman Library, 1994).

36. Stanford, Calif.: Stanford University Press, 2009.

37. The best Hebrew edition is that of Yosef Ben-Shlomo (Jerusalem: Mossad Bialik, 1981). The English translation I recommend is by Avi Weinstein (San Francisco: HarperCollins, 1994).

38. Lawrence Fine, ed., *Safed Spirituality: Rules of Mystical Piety*, Classics of Western Spirituality (Mahwah, N.J.: Paulist Press, 1984).

39. *Isaiah Horowitz: Generations of Adam*, trans. by Miles Krassen, Classics of Western Spirituality (Mahwah, N.J.: Paulist Press, 1996).

40. Albany: SUNY Press, 1989.

41. London: Valentine-Mitchell, 1960.

42. *The Song of Songs*, JPS Bible Commentary (Philadelphia: Jewish Publication Society, 2015).

43. Jerusalem: Sheviley Orḥot ha-Ḥayyim, 1992.

44. 3 vols., trans. by Eliyahu Munk (Jerusalem: Urim, 2000).

45. Woodstock, Vt.: Jewish Lights, 2013.

46. *The Religious Thought of Hasidism: Text and Commentary* (Hoboken, N.J.: Ktav, 1999).

47. New York: Behrman House, 1983.

48. Trans. by Jonathan Chipman (Princeton: Princeton University Press, 1993).

49. Trans. by Jeffrey M. Green (Albany: SUNY Press, 1993).

50. Jerusalem: Urim, 2008.

51. Princeton: Princeton University Press, 2016.

52. *Menahem Nahum of Chernobyl: Upright Practices, The Light of the Eyes,* Classics of Western Spirituality (Mahwah, N.J.: Paulist Press, 1982).

53. *The Language of Truth: The Torah Commentary of the* Sefat Emet, *Rabbi Yehudah Leib Alter of Ger,* trans. and interpreted by Arthur Green (Philadelphia: Jewish Publication Society, 1998).

54. Woodstock, Vt.: Jewish Lights, 1993.

55. Louisville, Ky.: Fons Vitae, 2011.

56. *All Is in the Hands of Heaven* (Hoboken, N.J.: Ktav, 1989).

57. *Hasidism on the Margin* (Madison, Wis.: University of Wisconsin Press, 2003).

58. *The Holy Fire* (Northvale, N.J.: Jason Aronson, 1994).

59. Bloomington: Indiana University Press, 1970.

60. Trans. by Stephen Jolly (Northvale, N.J.: Jason Aronson, 1993).

61. *Wrapped in a Holy Flame: Teachings and Tales of the Hasidic Masters* (San Francisco: Jossey-Bass, 2003).

62. *Nahman of Bratslav: Tales,* trans. by Arnold Band, Classics of Western Spirituality (Mahwah, N.J.: Paulist Press, 1978).

63. *The Seven Beggars & Other Kabbalistic Tales of Rebbe Nachman of Breslov* and *The Lost Princess & Other Kabbalistic Tales of Rebbe Nachman of Breslov,* trans. by Aryeh Kaplan (Woodstock, Vt.: Jewish Lights, 2005).

64. Woodstock, Vt.: Jewish Lights, 1992.

About Jewish Lights

People of all faiths and backgrounds yearn for books that attract, engage, educate, and spiritually inspire.

Our principal goal is to stimulate thought and help all people learn about who the Jewish People are, where they come from, and what the future can be made to hold. While people of our diverse Jewish heritage are the primary audience, our books speak to people in the Christian world as well and will broaden their understanding of Judaism and the roots of their own faith.

We bring to you authors who are at the forefront of spiritual thought and experience. While each has something different to say, they all say it in a voice that you can hear.

Our books are designed to welcome you and then to engage, stimulate, and inspire. We judge our success not only by whether or not our books are beautiful and commercially successful, but by whether or not they make a difference in your life.

For your information and convenience, at the back of this book we have provided a list of other Jewish Lights books you might find interesting and useful. They cover all the categories of your life:

Bar/Bat Mitzvah	Life Cycle
Bible Study / Midrash	Meditation
Children's Books	Men's Interest
Congregation Resources	Parenting
Current Events / History	Prayer / Ritual / Sacred Practice
Ecology / Environment	Social Justice
Fiction: Mystery, Science Fiction	Spirituality
Grief / Healing	Theology / Philosophy
Holidays / Holy Days	Travel
Inspiration	Twelve Steps
Kabbalah / Mysticism / Enneagram	Women's Interest

RABBI ARTHUR GREEN, PhD, is recognized as one of the world's preeminent authorities on Jewish thought and spirituality. He is rector of the Rabbinical School and the Irving Brudnick Professor of Philosophy and Religion at Hebrew College. Professor emeritus at Brandeis University, he also taught at the University of Pennsylvania and the Reconstructionist Rabbinical College, where he served as dean and president. Dr. Green is author of *Ehyeh: A Kabbalah for Tomorrow; Seek My Face: A Jewish Mystical Theology; Tormented Master: The Life and Spiritual Quest of Rabbi Nahman of Bratslav; These Are the Words: A Vocabulary of Jewish Spiritual Life* (all Jewish Lights); *A Guide to the Zohar* (Stanford University Press); *The Language of Truth: The Torah Commentary of the Sefat Emet* (Jewish Publication Society); and *Radical Judaism* (Yale University Press). He is coeditor of *Your Word Is Fire: The Hasidic Masters on Contemplative Prayer* and a contributor to *My People's Passover Haggadah: Traditional Texts, Modern Commentaries*, edited by Rabbi Lawrence A. Hoffman, PhD, and David Arnow, PhD (both Jewish Lights). He lectures widely at universities and in Jewish communities throughout North America, as well as in Israel, where he visits each year.

....

"Mines the tradition for modern believers, marrying its insights with science and other disciplines."
—Boston Globe

"Uniquely combines genuine mastery of the subject matter with great common sense, lucidity and, of special significance, a serious commitment to the practical value of Jewish mysticism in modern life."
—The Jerusalem Report

"Green is a formidable teacher of Jewish mysticism, and this volume amplifies and deepens the insights and wisdom contained in his previous work, *These Are the Words.*"
—Spirituality & Health

....

Speaking Torah
Spiritual Teachings from around the Maggid's Table

By Arthur Green, with Ebn Leader, Ariel Evan Mayse and Or N. Rose
The most powerful Hasidic teachings made accessible—from some of the world's preeminent authorities on Jewish thought and spirituality.

6 x 9, Hardcover
Volume 1: 512 pp, 978-1-58023-668-3
Volume 2: 448 pp, 978-1-58023-694-2

Tormented Master
The Life and Spiritual Quest of Rabbi Nahman of Bratslav

By Arthur Green
Explores the inner torments and religious quest of one of Hasidism's major figures, providing an important key to making his teachings accessible.

6 x 9, 416 pp, Quality PB, 978-1-879045-11-8

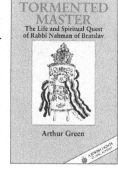

Your Word Is Fire
The Hasidic Masters on Contemplative Prayer

Edited and translated with a new introduction by Arthur Green and Barry W. Holtz

Through advice, parables and explanations, the Hasidic masters of the past speak to our own attempts to find meaning in prayer.
6 x 9, 160 pp, Quality PB, 978-1-879045-25-5

Printed in the USA
CPSIA information can be obtained
at www.ICGtesting.com
JSHW012027140824
68134JS00033B/2919